In the Master's Hands

REV. BRUCE PERO

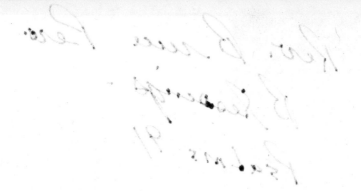

◆ FriesenPress

One Printers Way
Altona, MB R0G 0B0
Canada

www.friesenpress.com

ISBN
978-1-03-917841-0 (Hardcover)
978-1-03-917840-3 (Paperback)
978-1-03-917842-7 (eBook)

1. RELIGION, BIBLICAL MEDITATIONS

Distributed to the trade by The Ingram Book Company

TABLE OF CONTENTS

Chapter 1
My Remnant Church   1

Chapter 2
Because Of The Cross   5

Chapter 3
I Never Knew You   9

Chapter 4
We Need the Holy Spirit   17

Chapter 5
The Hope We Have in Jesus   23

Chapter 6
In The Master's Hands   29

Chapter 7
Life Through the Spirit   33

Chapter 8
Importance of the Name Jesus   41

Chapter 9
Strike The Rock   45

Chapter 10
We Are Called to Praise God   51

Chapter 11
Does God Know Me?   55

Chapter 12
Heart Felt words   59

Chapter 13
Love   63

Chapter 14
Someday 73

Chapter 15
Redeemed 81

Chapter 16
The End-Time Plan 85

Chapter 17
My Creator, A Worthy Confidant 91

Chapter 18
End Times Revelation Eight 99

Chapter 19
Light Of the Spirit 105

Chapter 20
The Gate Keepers 109

Chapter 21
The Reality of Redemption 115

Chapter 22
The Word Coming Alive in Us 121

Chapter 23
Judged And Condemned 129

Chapter 24
A New Commandment I Give You 133

Chapter 25
The Lamb of God 137

Chapter 26
Overcoming the Weakness of Fear of Sickness 141

Chapter 27
Abandoned But Not Forsaken 145

Chapter 28
The Holy Spirit is in You 151

INTRODUCTION

As I contemplate the introduction of this second book, I can't do it without thanking my wife for being such an inspiration and Carol stood by me for forty-seven years. When writing this book I wanted to share the teachings, In The Master's Hands, to make a difference in others' lives, as they did in mine. Each time I wrote another chapter, I would put my study books and my bible out in front of me. Then I would lay my hands on them and pray, Lord what would you have me to say in this message to your people today?

So you see I was the instrument but God is the author and finisher of all good works. I pray each chapter blesses your hearts. Amen!!!

Rev. Bruce Pero

DEDICATION

To my home church where I started my ministry.

I give thanks to my heavenly Father, the Holy Spirit, and my Lord Jesus Christ for the supernatural help I received in writing this book. Also thanks to Carol Jeffrey Pero who went home to be with her Lord and Savior on May 9th, 2018, for her inspiration. Thanks to Carol Switzer Pero for helping me complete this book's writing.

Praise be to God.
Rev Bruce Pero

CHAPTER 1
My Remnant Church

As I prayed over what title I should write about next, the Lord instilled in my heart these words. My Remnant Church. I thought, what could these words mean? So, I began to ask for clarification, and also, I started looking into the meaning of remnant in God's word. Look what I found! Isaiah 46:3-4 "Listen to Me," [says the Lord], "O house of Jacob, and all the remnant of the house of Israel, you who have been carried by Me from your birth and have been carried [in My arms] from the womb,

4 Even to your old age I am He, and even to your advanced old age, I will carry you! I have made you, and I will carry you; Be assured I will carry you and I will save you."

From the beginning of time, God has had a remnant of His people; a small nucleus of people He has held together as His people for the end-time creation of His church. If you doubt what I say, check out what Jeremiah 23:3 tells us. "Then I will gather the remnant of My flock out of all the countries to which I have driven them and bring them back to their folds and pastures, and they will be fruitful and multiply." ROMANS 9:29 It is as Isaiah foretold, "If the Lord of Hosts had not left us seed [future generations from which a believing remnant of Israelite came], we would have become like Sodom, and would have resembled Gomorrah [totally rejected and destroyed]!" Romans 11:05 So too then, at the present time there has come to be a remnant [a small believing minority] according to God's gracious choice.

Now what we have just written has been an outline of God's plan for His chosen people.

But this is only the beginning of His church, of His bride that He will call to the marriage supper of the Lamb.

Revelation 19:9 Then the angel said to me, "Write, 'Blessed are those who are invited to the Marriage Supper of the Lamb.'" And he said to me [further], "These are the true and exact words of God."

(Let's break this down. The Marriage Supper is when the saints, all the people who have accepted Christ as their Lord and Savior are caught up in Heaven to be with Jesus for eternity, Jew and Gentile. This is a great celebration that will take place in Heaven around the throne of God, with the Lamb, which is referring to Jesus being the Lamb that was slain for the sins of the world. What an amazing, glorious day that is going to be. You won't want to miss it. Amen!!)

Ephesians 2:6-7,16, "And He raised us up together with Him and made us sit down together [giving us joint seating with Him] in the heavenly sphere [by our being] in Christ Jesus (the Messiah, the Anointed One). 7 He did this that He might clearly demonstrate through the ages to come the immeasurable (limitless, surpassing) riches of His free Grace (His unmerited favor) in [His] kindness and goodness of heart toward us in Christ Jesus.

16 And [He designed] to reconcile to God both [Jew and Gentile, united] in a single body using His cross, thereby killing the mutual enmity and bringing the feud to an end. The scripture clearly says, "He raised us up together to be seated with Him in the Heavenly sphere." The only reference to the people that will join Him is found in Ephesians 2:16, speaking of the Jew and Gentile.

So, the point I'm trying to make is if you go to Heaven, don't look for any other religious groups, you won't find them.

There won't be any man-made religions, or someone saying come over here we are the answer to getting into heaven; don't look for any religious organizations because there won't be one.

Jesus made it very clear when He was here on this earth who had the right answer. Look in, John 14:6 Jesus said to him, "I am the Way and the Truth and the Life; no one comes to the Father except by (through) Me." (So, no organization, or religious group, can get you into Heaven except the saving Grace and intimate relationship with our Lord and Savior Jesus Christ.

So, the Remnant that is talked about in God's Word, the Remnant that He will make His church from, the Remnant that will be called to the great marriage supper of the Lamb is all the believers that have accepted Jesus Christ as their Lord and Savior and worship Him in Spirit and in Truth. Matthew 16:18 "And I say to you that you are Peter, and on this rock, I will build My church; and the gates of Hades (death) will not overpower it [by preventing the resurrection of the Christ]." John 4:23 "But a time is coming and is already here when the true worshipers will worship the Father in spirit [from the heart, the inner self] and in truth; for the Father seeks such people to be His worshipers." So as Jesus spoke to Peter about building His church, we can be part of that Remnant to build His church. The criteria for this are that we have an intimate relationship with Christ, and we are to worship Him in spirit and in truth. I pray to see you all in Heaven. Amen!!!

04/05/2021
Rev Bruce Pero

CHAPTER 2
Because Of The Cross

Theologians have taught about it, pastors have preached great messages about it, and evangelists have moved the hearts of the masses with their pointed descriptions of it, but let's just look at what has happened because of the cross. One question for you and me, where would we be spiritual if it were not for what took place on the cross? Would we even be thinking about or concerned about where we would be spending eternity? Perhaps eternity or even our life after we die would be something that would cross our minds. After all, if there had not been a cross, how would we know about the saving Grace of our Lord and Savior and soon-coming King? We often ask why did there have to be a cross at all? Let's see what God's word tells us and see if we can shed some light on these questions. For all the skeptics who will say, this was for those days, but it does not really apply to our situation today; have I got news for you? Follow me as I go back through God's word and try to paint a picture of the cross. Isaiah 53 Amplified Bible, Classic Edition

53 "Who has believed (trusted in, relied upon, and clung to) our message [of that which was revealed to us]? And to whom has the arm of the Lord been revealed?"

(In Isaiah 53:1t tells us how the Israelite people clung to and relied on God's leading; after all, they were God's chosen people.) 2 "For [the Servant of God] grew up before Him like a tender plant, and like a root out of the dry ground; He has no form or comeliness [royal, kingly pomp], that we should look at Him and no beauty that we should desire Him."

(Even back in Isaiah they were referring to the person and the life of Christ.

He was described as not good-looking but plain, as we would call it; just an ordinary man.)

3 "He was despised and rejected and forsaken by men, a Man of sorrows and pains, and acquainted with grief and sickness; and like One from Whom men hide their faces He was despised, and we did not appreciate His worth or have any esteem for Him."

(This was a message given, by prophesying and describing how the children of Israel were close to God. How God was going to send the Messiah and that Jesus would look like any common man, taking away the infirmities and sins of the world.)

4 "Surely He has borne our griefs (sicknesses, weaknesses, and distresses) and carried our sorrows and pains [of punishment], yet we [ignorantly] considered Him stricken, smitten, and afflicted by God [as if with leprosy]."

(If it were not for the cross all of these things could not have been accomplished, but remember this vision was given seven hundred years before Jesus was even born. In short, Jesus was dying on the cross for your sins and mine. The Apostle Paul said that Jesus "loved me and gave Himself for me". 5 "But He was wounded for our transgressions, He was bruised for our guilt and iniquities; the chastisement [needful to obtain] peace and well-being for us was upon Him, and with the stripes [that wounded] Him we are healed and made whole."

So, you see, even in the time of the Old Testament, God had a plan for the salvation of the world. God's plan always was to rid the world of sin, sickness, and disease. But to do that, there had to be a sacrifice, speaking figuratively Jesus was to be the last sacrifice, the last lamb sacrificed for our sins. That's where the cross comes into play.

Isaiah 53:7 "He was oppressed, [yet when] He was afflicted, He was submissive and opened not His mouth; like a lamb that is led to the slaughter, and as a sheep before her shearers are dumb, so He opened not His mouth."

(All of this is leading up to the cross and its significance of it. Jesus knew the plan of the Father and did not say or do anything that would change or jeopardize God's plan. The devil thought he had won when he saw Jesus die on the cross. Little did he know it was just the beginning of his own defeat. 1 John 3:14 "Just as Moses lifted up the serpent in the desert [on a pole], so must [so] the Son of Man must be lifted up [on the cross],"

John 8;28 So Jesus added, "When you have lifted up the Son of Man [on the cross], you will realize (know, understand) that I am He [for Whom you look] and that I do nothing of Myself (of My own accord or on My own authority), but I say [exactly] what My Father has taught Me".

Because of the cross, we have that assurance that the sacrifice was made for the forgiveness of our sins. When Jesus died on the cross, He took upon Himself all of the sins for you and me, giving us the assurance of eternal life with our Lord and Savior in Heaven. It sure beats the alternative, and achieving this promise is really simple. Ask Jesus to be Lord of your life and ask Him to forgive you of all your sins. Believing He gave His life for you, and three days later He arose from the grave and ascended to Heaven. If you have done this you are on your way to Heaven, study his word and do your best to live for Him. I look forward to seeing you in Heaven. Amen!!!!!

April 3/2021
Rev Bruce Pero

CHAPTER 3
I Never Knew You

A question asked down through the ages of time that most people have, difficulty answering. This question has quite often stumped many theologians and scholars. The question is simply this, why would God say, "I never knew you?" How could a caring, loving God allow people He created to spend an eternity in endless torment in Hell? So, let's take a look at this and see if we can shed some light on this topic through the help of the Holy Spirit. You see I would never try answering this type of question without the help of the Holy Spirit.

Scriptures, there is a scripture that is most commonly quoted when we are discussing this topic, and the quote is found in Matthew 7:21 "Not everyone that saith unto me, Lord, Lord, shall enter into the kingdom of heaven; but he that doth the will of my Father which is in heaven. (When it refers to, he or those that do the Father's will, His commandments, His precepts, this is referring to those that have an intimate relationship with our Lord and Savior.) 22 Many will say to me in that day, "Lord, Lord, have we not prophesied in thy name? and in thy name have cast out devils? and in thy name done many wonderful works?" When referring to, many will say to me that day, this is referring to the return of Jesus and the day is when we go to be with the Lord in Heaven. These people will be trying to explain how and why Jesus should know and recognize them, but again without that personal relationship with Christ in our hearts, He will not recognize or welcome us. Here we see how the children of Israel were crying out for mercy from their God, whom they thought had abandoned them.

They, like many of us, thought our good works would give us a place in heaven for eternity, but this is what God's word has to say about that idea.

Isaiah 64:6 "For we all have become like one who is [ceremonially] unclean [like a leper], And all our deeds of righteousness are like filthy rags; We all wither and decay like a leaf, and our wickedness [our sin, our injustice, our wrongdoing], like the wind, takes us away [carrying us far from God's favor, toward destruction]."

Matthew 15:8 "These people draw near me with their mouths and honor me with their lips, but their hearts hold off and are far away from me." Many are doing and have done wonderful works in Christ's name, but it has been for their own agenda, not to glorify the Father as His word tells us we are to do but to advance their own cause.

Matthew 7;23 "And then will I profess unto them, I never knew you: depart from me, ye that work iniquity." (When Jesus says, "depart from me, ye that work Iniquity," Jesus is basically telling you who lived sinful lives but tried to give the impression you were serving me, but you were serving yourselves and Satan. On that day of judgment, Jesus will cast those people, who never had an intimate relationship with Him, out to spend eternity with Satan in the lake of fire. But before all of this is to take place, we need to remember that Christ has given and is giving us so many opportunities to have an intimate relationship with him, as our Lord and soon-coming King.

For example, we read in, John 14:22-23, "Judas, not Iscariot, asked Him, Lord, how is it that You will reveal Yourself [make Yourself real] to us and not to the world?"

23 Jesus answered, "If a person [really] loves Me, he will keep My word [obey My teaching]; and My Father will love him, and We will come to him and make Our home (abode, special dwelling place) with him."

You see, "It is not God's will that any should perish but all should come to repentance."

(2 Peter 3:9) It is not God's will that anyone should be lost but all would come to know Him and spend eternity in heaven, with our Lord.

Matthew 18:11-14, "For the son of man came to save [from the penalty of eternal death] that which was lost".12 "What do you think? If a man has a hundred sheep, and one of them has gone astray and gets lost, will he not leave the ninety-nine on the mountain and go in search of the one that is lost?"

13 "And if it should be that he finds it, truly I say to you, he rejoices more over it than over the ninety-nine that did not get lost. 14 Just so it is not the will of My Father Who is

in heaven that one of these little ones (or Persons) should be lost and perish."

Remember what Jesus said in John 13:34-35 "I am giving you a new commandment, that you love one another. Just as I have loved you, so you too are to love one another. By this everyone will know that you are My disciples if you have love and unselfish concern for one another." This is not just a commandment for us to follow, it is a heartfelt intimacy that Jesus offers to us when He says, "Just as I have loved you, so you too are to love one another." The Bible tells us that God knew us before we were formed in our mother's womb. Psalm 139:13 For "You formed my innermost parts; You knit me [together] in my mother's womb. So, if He had that much interest in us, to know us before we were created do you not think His plan was for us to be with Him in Heaven?

Also, He would give his only son as a sacrifice on the cross for our sins so we could be saved from an eternity in Hell. Again, I want to emphasize to all that it was not God's plan or intent that He would say to depart from me (I Never Knew You.)

Ephesians 1:5, For He foreordained us (destined us, planned in love for us) to be adopted (revealed) as His own children through Jesus Christ, by the purpose of His will [because it pleased Him and was His kind intent.]

You know when we get married and start our families we hope and plan for the best in our children's lives. But who are we kidding, it does not always turn out the way we planned or hoped for. Proverbs 22:6 "Train up a child in the way he should go: and when he is old, he will not depart from it."

The children have choices to make, as we did. They do not think the same as mom or dad because we all have different personalities, thus the outcome of our decisions will be different. This was God's plan that everyone would make their own choices in life, whether to serve Him and have an intimate relationship with Jesus or to walk away from Him and serve the world or Satan. All we, as parents can do is what God tells us in His instruction of His word.

But let me tell you in most cases when children are given a good foundation of God's word, they may stray from it for some time but in most cases, they will return before they leave this world.

We can only do our best, then put them in God's hands and let Him take care of them. People again say it is not God's will that He would have to say, "depart from me I never knew you."

But by the choice we make not to serve Him, also refusing to have an intimate relationship with Him, and denying His very existence, we are forcing God to say depart from me I never knew you. 1 Corinthians 1:21 For when the world with all its earthly wisdom failed to perceive and recognize and know God using its own philosophy, God in His wisdom was pleased through the foolishness of preaching [salvation, procured by Christ and to be had through Him], to save those who believed (who clung to and trusted in and relied on Him).

You know people we have lost two generations, maybe more to the attitude of, I'm not going to tell my children how they are to live and what they should believe. When they get old enough, they can make up their own minds. Shame on us for being so lazy and uncaring.

If our children were to put their hands near a flame, would we not pull them away from it, or tell them that is going to burn them? When it comes to life in eternity, we shirk our duties as parents. We either don't believe there is a God who is going to Judge us for our actions, or we just take the attitude, I don't have time for that stuff, I'll let the pastor or someone else explain all that stuff to them.

In the meantime, our children and, we are heading to a flame that will burn us forever, it is referred to as the lake of fire, better known as Hell, where we will spend eternity without the saving knowledge of Jesus Christ.

2 Timothy 3:1-3 Amplified Bible, Classic Edition 1 "But understand this, that in the last days will come (set in) perilous times of great stress and trouble [hard to deal with and hard to bear]."

2 For people will be lovers of self and [utterly] self-centered, lovers of money and aroused by an inordinate [greedy] desire for wealth, proud and arrogant and contemptuous boasters. They will be abusive (blasphemous, scoffing), disobedient to parents, ungrateful, unholy, and profane. 3 "[They will be] without natural [human] affection (callous and inhuman), relentless (admitting of no truce or appeasement); [they will be] slanderers (false accusers, troublemakers), intemperate and loose in morals and conduct, uncontrolled and fierce, haters of good." 2 Corinthians 2:17 Amplified Bible, Classic Edition 17 "For we are not, like so many, [like hucksters making a trade of] peddling God's Word [shortchanging and

adulterating the divine message]; but like [men] of sincerity and the purest motive, as [commissioned and sent] by God, we speak [His message] in Christ (the Messiah),

in the [very] sight and presence of God." So, in closing, I ask you one question. If you were to die in the next few hours or days, do you know where you will spend eternity? Whether you chose to believe it or not there is a Heaven to gain and a Hell to shun (or avoid), what will you choose this day?

John 3:16 Amplified Bible, Classic Edition 16 "For God so greatly loved and dearly prized the world that He even] gave up His only begotten Son, so that whoever believes in (trusts in, clings to, relies on) He shall not perish (come to destruction, be lost) but have eternal (everlasting) life." My prayer is that you would accept Jesus Christ as your Lord and Savior, and on that day when we stand in heaven for eternity, I will be able to look around and see you standing there with me. Love and Blessings.

Rev Bruce Pero
March 31/2021

CHAPTER 4
We Need the Holy Spirit

We need the gifts of the Holy Spirit. We cannot say that we do not need any of them or that we are limited to having one or two of them operating in our ministering and lives. The fact is that we need them all. We must avail ourselves of them, which is to make use of them. The Holy Spirit is the author of all nine gifts, and He resides inside every believer. So the capacity or potential is there for every believer to operate as God intends and thereby bless others. (Read 1 Corinthians 6-13)

When writing about the spiritual gifts in 1 Corinthians 12, Paul explained that the gifts are given to every man as the Spirit wills (vs. 11). God is saying that these gifts have been given to every believer.

The Holy Spirit's gifts are like equipment. Some people might not like for me to refer to these gifts as equipment, but a spiritual gift is something that is utilized by God to work at a certain time.

No one sends a worker to dig ditches without a shovel or the kind of equipment he would need to get the job done. It would be unjust and unfair for God to demand that you do a job without giving you the capacity, potential, authority, power, and necessary equipment to get it done. The Lord is not unfair or unjust. He has given us the gifts of the Holy Spirit so that we can accomplish what He has called us to do.

God has called every believer to go into the entire world and preach the gospel to every creature, to heal the sick, raise the dead, and cast out devils (Mark 16:15-16). Since He has given us a job to do, He has also given us the equipment to get that job done.

Verse 31 of 1 Corinthians 12 says that we are to covet earnestly the best gifts. What is the best gift? The one that is better by far and the highest of them all is Love.

1 Corinthians 12:3 says, wherefore I give you to understand, that no man speaking by the Spirit of God called Jesus accursed: and that no man can say that Jesus is the Lord but by the Holy Spirit. It takes the Holy Spirit in everything we do. We cannot even say Jesus is Lord, without the Holy Spirit's Help. If we don't become aware of the Holy Spirit and learn how He functions, we will have difficulty accomplishing anything for God.

The Holy Spirit is supposed to work through the body of Christ. He didn't quit working through God's people when the original twelve disciples died. The acts of the Holy Spirit didn't end with the last scripture in the Book of Acts.

Paul wrote, and my speech and my preaching were not with enticing words of man's wisdom, but in demonstration of the Spirit and of power, (1 Corinthians 2:4). Paul knew that he needed the Holy Spirit to fulfill his ministry. So do we.

We know that Jesus lives in the life of every believer. And He still lives to destroy the works of the devil, but now He does it through us.

We know that Satan has some miraculous power that is designed to steal, kill, and destroy, but Jesus said in Mathew 28: 18, "All authority (all power) has been given to me in heaven and on earth." Today, He exercises His authority over the devil through His saints. Luke10:19 tells us what Jesus is saying to the church, "Behold, I give unto you power (delegated power) to tread on serpents and scorpions and over all the power (dunamous- miraculous power) of the enemy: and nothing shall by any means hurt you."

We can exercise or demonstrate that power and authority over the demonic realm.

We need this power or anointing of God if we are going to set people free. The anointing of God is simply God in your flesh doing what you cannot possibly do.

Ephesians 3:20 says, "Now to Him who can do exceedingly, abundantly above all that we ask or think, according to the power that works in us."

He wants to use you to set others free.

The anointing that God put upon Jesus was the presence and power of God manifested. The word manifest means to make evident, in our context, it can mean to bring out of the Spiritual world into the physical world. Every time Jesus obeyed His Father, the anointing of God was releasing power from the spiritual world into our world. That power was the Person of the Holy Spirit. Without His ability to work through us, our work is unacceptable.

The Bible says, "It is neither by might nor by power but by My, Spirit says the Lord of hosts." The works we plan and carry out from our own fleshly minds are unacceptable to the Lord. Only the works of the spirit -only what the Holy Spirit initiates -will He Bless.

The only way to keep the devil out is to stay filled with the Holy Spirit.

Paul went on to admonish his readers in Ephesians 5:17-18, "Understand what the will of the Lord is; do not be drunk with wine but be filled with the Spirit." The word filled is in the continual sense: of always being filled. In other words, you can have many Pentecosts and be filled again and again. You can ask the Lord to fill you right now. Say, Lord, your Word says in Psalms 92:10 that you caused the psalmist's horn to be exalted like a wild ox, and you anointed him with fresh oil (which is a symbol of the Holy Spirit), so will you fill me right now with this fresh oil! Now thank Jesus for filling you with the Holy Spirit.

We have ministers today who cannot relax after a meeting until they have their glass of wine or a can of beer.

Jesus said, "Do not be drunk with wine, but be filled with the Holy Spirit." Be filled with the Holy Spirit before the meeting, during the meeting, and after the meeting. AMEN It is possible to stay filled by praying in tongues. Never be satisfied with where you are right now. There is always more, much more. Also, the anointing can increase upon your life; the anointing of God can be measured. Elisha had twice as much as Elijah. 2 Kings 2:9. You are the only one who sets the limit or boundary. John the Baptist spoke of Jesus in these terms: For since He whom God has sent speaks the words of God (proclaims God's own message) God does not give Him His Spirit sparingly or by measure, but boundless is the gift God makes of His Spirit. There is no stopping place with Jesus. The Bible says that we can receive from the Spirit without measure John 3:34, to the baptismal measure, Matt 3:11, to the fullness of God Eph. 3:19, to the river of living waters, John 7:37-39, and finally to the full anointing of the Spirit, endued with power from on high, Luke 24:49. Every time the (dunamois, dynamic, or dynamite) power comes upon you, there is an increase of anointing in your life, and the impossible becomes possible. When Jesus was about to ascend into heaven, He made it clear how He would not leave the disciples all alone as we read in, John 14:16 "And I will ask the Father, and He will give you another Helper (Comforter, Advocate, Intercessor—Counselor, Strengthener, Standby), to be with you forever." 17 the Spirit of Truth, whom the world cannot receive [and take to its heart] because it does not see Him or know Him, but you know Him because He (the Holy Spirit) remains with you continually and will be in you. 18 "I will not leave you as orphans [comfortless, bereaved, and helpless]; I will come [back] to you."

Rev Bruce Pero.

CHAPTER 5
The Hope We Have in Jesus

As I grew up on the farm, as a child, it was always instilled in us that we had hope in Jesus; 1 Corinthians 1;7 that we are not [consciously] falling behind or lacking in any special spiritual endowment or Christian grace. The reception of which is due to the power of divine grace operating in your souls by the Holy Spirit], while you wait and watch [constantly living in hope] for the coming of our Lord Jesus Christ and [His] being made visible to all.

While attending Sunday school every Sunday we were taught to pray and follow the golden rule. So even in my later years, those same rules are very important to me. I feel compelled to add this insert to my writing. We have lost approximately two generations out of the church. Young parents came up with the notion, that we'll just let the children do what they want as long as they don't get into trouble. When they get older, they can make up their own minds about church attendance and Jesus. My answer to that idea is shame on us for shirking our responsibility.

Whatever happened to, Proverbs 22:6 "Train up a child in the way he should go [teaching him to seek God's wisdom and will for his abilities and talents], Even when he is old, he will not depart from it."

It is time we get back to the principles that God laid out for us since the beginning of time. Amen!

I have seen friends come and go but you know the one true friend I have has never left me nor forsaken me. Hebrews 13:5 "Let your conversation be without covetousness; and be content with such things as ye have: for he hath said, I will never leave thee, nor forsake thee."

Whenever life got difficult through sickness in my own body, or the loss of a loved one, my friend Jesus Christ has always been right there beside me.

One of His golden rules is found in Matthew 7:7,8. "Keep on asking and it will be given you; keep on seeking and you will find; keep on knocking [reverently] and [the door] will be opened to you. 8 For everyone who keeps on asking receives; and he who keeps on seeking finds; and to him who keeps on knocking, [the door] will be opened." The term reverently knowing is to show reverence and respect to our Lord and Savior, but also remember Jesus said, "We can come boldly into the throne room of God."

Hebrews 4:16 "Let us, therefore, come boldly unto the throne of grace, that we may obtain mercy, and find grace to help in time of need."

The hope we actually have in Jesus is whether we choose to believe in Him or not, to believe is to have hope.

But before we depart from this world, we have a major decision to make. Now some people would say, well I don't have any decision to make because I'm going with all my friends. That's all well and good but do you know where your friends will spend eternity?

Then there's the old idea that I have always been a good person; I have done what I could to help others so I should go to Heaven. Please listen to me, I can stand in a garage but that does not make me a car.

We remember what is written in Isaiah 64:6 Amplified Bible 6 "For we all have become like one who is [ceremonially] unclean [like a leper], And all our deeds of righteousness are like filthy rags;" We all wither and decay like grass, and our wickedness [our sin, our injustice, our wrongdoing], like the wind, takes us away [carrying us far from God's favor, toward destruction].

Here's what God's word tells us also in, Romans 3:23 "For all have sinned, and come short of the glory of God;"

Matthew 7:13,14. "Enter through the narrow gate; for wide is the gate and spacious and broad is the way that leads away to destruction, and many are those who are entering through it.14 But the gate is narrow (contracted by pressure) and the way is straitened and compressed that leads away to life, and few are those who find it."

So, the hope that Jesus Christ offers us is the way to eternal life in Heaven, not an eternity in Hell.

Some people would say God is not so cruel that He would send us to an eternity in Hell. You are absolutely correct. That is why He said in Matthew 7;21 "Not everyone who says to Me, Lord, Lord, will enter the kingdom of heaven, but he who does the will of My Father Who is in heaven.

22 Many will say to Me on that day, "Lord, Lord, have we not prophesied in Your name and driven out demons in Your name and done many mighty works in Your name?"

23 And then I will say to them openly (publicly), "I never knew you; depart from Me, you who act wickedly [disregarding My commands]." Mark 7:6 "He replied, "Rightly did Isaiah prophesy about you hypocrites (play-actors, pretenders), as it is written [in Scripture], these people honor Me with their lips, but their heart is far from Me."

(Without accepting Jesus Christ as your Lord and Savior you will not see heaven, Jesus will say, you have not lived a life of intimacy with me, (Jesus), so He is going to say depart from me I never knew you. God's word is very clear in that He wants everyone to make it to Heaven, but He gives us that choice of where we will spend eternity.

John 3:16 "For God so greatly loved and dearly prized the world that He [even] gave up His only begotten (unique) Son, so that whoever believes in (trusts in, clings to, relies on) He shall not perish (come to destruction, be lost) but have eternal (everlasting) life."

The hope we have in Jesus is that He gave His own life so that we could spend eternity with Him in Heaven. What a hope, to know we have a better life after we leave this world.

John said it best, in Philippians 3:14 "I press on toward the goal to win the [supreme and heavenly] prize to which God in Christ Jesus is calling us upward."

So, I pray you too know where your hope lies. I pray it is in Christ Jesus. My hope is that I will see you all in Heaven. Amen!!

Rev Bruce Pero

CHAPTER 6
In The Master's Hands

When Paul was first introduced to Christianity, he was very rebellious, like so many of us that are professing to be Christians today. The same as Paul, many of us have to have a road to Damascus experience before we can grasp the true meaning of holding onto the master's hand. Acts 9:3 "Now, as he traveled on, he came near to Damascus, and suddenly a light from heaven flashed around him, 4 And he fell to the ground. Then he heard a voice saying to him, Saul, Saul, why are you persecuting Me [harassing, troubling, and molesting Me]?" How many times have we made fun of those who came to know Jesus persecuted and made fun of those who followed Jesus or went to church? Were we not of that very same religious mentality as Saul? It wasn't until Saul had this experience on the road to Damascus with Jesus that he gave his life to the Lord, and shortly after changed His name to Paul. Thus, we have Paul the apostle. This is why Paul was able to write many books of the Bible. It was because Saul/Paul's life was in the master's hands. If we are willing, we too can know what it is like to be in the master's hands. But one of Paul's most astounding statements was best written in Romans 1:16 "For I am not ashamed of the Gospel (good news) of Christ, for it is God's power working unto salvation [for deliverance from eternal death] to everyone who believes with a personal trust and a confident surrender and firm reliance, to the Jew first and also to the Greek."

17 For in the Gospel a righteousness which God ascribes (or assigns to us), is revealed, both springing from faith and leading to faith [disclosed through the way of faith that arouses to more faith].

As it is written, the man who through faith is just and upright (in right standing with God), shall live and shall live by faith. What is faith you ask? Hebrews 11:1 The Triumphs of Faith. "Now faith is the assurance (title deed, confirmation) of things hoped for (divinely guaranteed), and the evidence of things not seen." [The conviction of their reality—faith comprehends as fact what cannot be experienced by the physical senses]. Have you had your Damascus Road experience with Jesus? Believe me when I say you will never be the same. To literally hold onto the Masters's hand and say, "I will not let go until you bless me," is knowing all about my Lord. I encourage you to try it. Take hold of the Masters's hand, draw close to Him and He will draw close to you because He loves us all with a never-ending love. Amen!

Romans 6:5(K J V), "For if we have been planted together in the likeness of his death, we shall be also in the likeness of His resurrection:" To make this a little clearer, in the same likeness, when you give up your sinful life you then go through death to your old way of living in sin. Then just as Christ was resurrected you are resurrected to a new life in and with Christ. As Christ died for us, He became one with us. He died for all mankind. He took everyone's place on the cross.

That means when He died, we died. We became one with Him on the cross and in His death. He did all this in our place because He was made a sin for us. Through His death upon the cross, we were made alive in Him." Our very life is possible only through Jesus' death on the cross. Through His death, He conquered sin, Satan, Hell, and the Grave. He became weak, so we can be strong. He became a sin, so we can be righteous. He became sick, so we can be healthy. He freed us from all the curses of spiritual death. We became one with Him as He became one with us. If you would like to know my Master, study God's word, and pray in the spirit, constantly.

He tells us, "If you draw near to me, I will draw near to you. "Psalm 73:28(K J V), "But as for me, it is good for me to draw near to God; I have made the Lord God my refuge and placed my trust in Him that I may tell of all Your works." If you want to know the Master and His love, always remember He wants to know you just as much, even more, because Jesus loves us with a never-ending love. Amen! Just reach out to Him. Just whisper the name of Jesus, Amen! 1 Corinthians 5:4 In the name of our Lord Jesus, when you are assembled, I am with you in spirit and with the power of our Lord Jesus. Romans 8:38-39 (K J V), "For I am persuaded, that neither death, nor life, nor angels, nor principalities, nor powers, nor things present, nor things to come." 39 Nor height, nor depth, nor any other creature, shall be able to separate us from the love of God, which is in Christ Jesus our Lord. They say to know someone is to walk a mile in their shoes or in this case, sandals. To know our Master is to be the hands and feet of Jesus in this world. In every situation in life just ask yourself, what would Jesus do? Then follow the leading of the Holy Spirit, that still small voice, you can't go wrong.

As I have said so many times, there is nothing you can do to make God love you anymore, and there's nothing you can do to make Him love you any less. Remember, He knew us before we were formed in our mother's womb. (Psalm 139:15) You are so very precious in His sight. Look what the Word has to say about each and every one of us in, Ephesians 2:10 (K J V), "For we are his workmanship, created in Christ Jesus unto good works, which God hath before ordained that we should walk in them."

Amen! My prayer for each and every one of us is that we can say, yes, I know the Master and He knows me. If you don't know my Jesus, I would be happy to introduce Him to you. Amen!

November 4/2016
Rev Bruce Pero

CHAPTER 7
Life Through the Spirit

In God's word we are told that He, (Jesus) or the Holy Spirit will not speak His own message or on His own authority; but He will tell whatever He hears from the Father. He will give the message that has been given to Him, and He will announce and declare to you the things that are to come or that will happen in the future. Also, in the same manner, the Holy Spirit will do the same as Jesus did, by doing and saying what the Father told him to do and speak. This is because Jesus, the Holy Spirit, and the Father are one; they are the most Holy Trinity. (They are one in purpose, one in direction, one in love.) John 16:14-15, Amplified Bible Version, Romans 8:1-11 Amplified Bible, we should not walk after the dictates of the flesh but after the dictates of the Spirit. Life in the Spirit is life, led by the Spirit and filled with the Spirit, and operating in and through the Holy Spirit. We have to see and believe that the Spirit is our guide, not our heads and emotions. We live by faith, not by sight. 2 Corinthians 5:7, (Amplified Bible), (It is so easy to listen to our emotions and follow them, but what is the Spirit telling me, should be the question we are all asking ourselves.)

A good example of this is Paul in Gal. 3:1-3, (Amplified Bible) Paul understood the importance of the power of the Spirit of God, and here we see that he is giving the Galatians a scolding or rebuke because, at one time, they believed in Him and were being led by the Spirit, but now they have gone back to listening to their emotions and forgetting about the Spirit.

Paul knew that the benefits of following the Spirit would profit them and make them successful in life. Paul knew also that when the spirit spoke, that was the final authority. Amen!! Galatians 1:15-17, (Amplified Bible), We need to remember as Paul wrote, that we were called before we were even born.

So, God's favor and grace are upon us and we are led by the Holy Spirit. We have been given the mandate to spread God's word; the good news to the lost and dying world. It is not necessary to confer with others, because our guidance and leading will come directly from God through His Holy Spirit. Paul didn't ask people about what he should or shouldn't do. He heard and knew it was the Spirit talking to him, and he obeyed the Spirit's still small voice. If we start to analyze what the Spirit is telling us, then we get into human reasoning and usually don't follow the Spirit. Paul did not fall into that trap. He heard the Spirit and did what the Spirit told him to do. Paul really understood how to live his life through or by the Spirit of God that was in him. It tells us in John 14:23, that Jesus answered, "If anyone [really] loves Me, he will keep My word (teaching); and My Father will love him, and We will come to him and make our dwelling place with him." We can be just like Paul by studying God's word, praying, and having fellowship with Him through the Holy Spirit. Romans 8:3-4, (Amplified Bible), The scripture tells us that the Law could not deal with man's sinful nature. But then God sent His own Son to be a sin offering for all of mankind. In doing so, God condemned sin for time and eternity. All we have to do is ask Him to forgive us of our sins, come into our hearts and be the Lord of our lives. Also, in doing this, God paid the ultimate price so that the righteous requirements of the law might be fully realized. We really need to know and remember, that we are a spirit, we have a soul, and we live in a body. This is how God made you. You will be surprised how often He, by the Holy Spirit, will speak into your spirit with direction for your prayers.

Don't just ask for things but praise Him; that is what we are here on this earth to do.

When you are praying and you sense the Holy Spirit moving in you, don't be afraid to open your mouth and let the Spirit speak through you, in that heavenly language. He tells us if we believe in Him, He will give us the desires of our hearts. All things are possible to him who believes. If He has promised it, and you can believe it, you can have it. Are you a believer? Then all things are possible to those who believe. AMEN. Jesus, as He was teaching the disciples and explaining what was to come in the future, told how demonic forces would try to change the truth through man-made religions. Some will not accept Christ and the Cross. Men will teach on their own merits, not being led by the guidance of the Holy Spirit. They will merely teach what tickles men's ears! Pastors will become more dependent on the number of people in their pews than on reaching souls for Christ. To some, it will be more important to have monetary gain; also, to have notoriety than to follow the leading of the Holy Spirit in their calling to minister.

Matthew 7:21-24 "Not everyone who says to Me, 'Lord, Lord,' will enter the kingdom of heaven, but only he who does the will of My Father who is in heaven. 22 Many will say to Me on that day [when I judge them], 'Lord, Lord, have we not prophesied in Your name, and driven out demons in Your name, and done many miracles in Your name?' 23 And then I will declare to them publicly, 'I never knew you; depart from Me [you are banished from My presence], you who act wickedly [disregarding My commands].'

If we would follow the direction of God and what He called us to do and have faith in Him, He would see our work accomplished; our churches would be full. Not only would churches be full, but the important thing would be that so many more could come to the saving knowledge of Jesus Christ.

Read in your Bible what it tells us about being vigilant in our walk with the Lord John 16:1-15 Amplified Bible. This is also referring to the end times and the anti-Christ.

There will come a time when people pick and choose what they wish to believe about God's word. They will only want to get their ears tickled with words that suit them. And they will even drive some believers out of the church because some will choose to believe the truth, the whole Bible not just parts of it. Let us look at 1 Timothy 4:1, (Amplified Bible), But the Holy Spirit distinctly and expressly declares, "That in later times, some will turn away from the faith, giving attention to deluding and seducing spirits and doctrines of demons," Jesus, throughout His teaching, was trying to warn the disciples of what was coming after He was gone. But, because of their love for Him, they were having a hard time understanding what Jesus was saying. This is also true today. Many people have a hard time grasping the true meaning of God's word. They don't understand when the Bible tells us we do battle against spirits and principalities in heavenly places. These are demonic forces. Jesus is telling the disciples, that He has to go so that the Holy Spirit will come. (Also, a finished work on the Cross was demanded of Christ before the Holy Spirit could be sent.) Just as the disciples could not understand what Jesus was telling them concerning the Holy Spirit, Christians today, still have difficulty grasping or understanding the workings of the Holy Spirit. People need to understand that when we accept Jesus as our Lord, He becomes a part of us. Jesus' spirit essentially becomes a part of our spirit, but not only that but then the Holy Spirit comes to dwell in us as well. The Holy Spirit is to be our guide in life, to be our advocate, our counselor, our adviser, and our go-to, in times of trouble. What Jesus is referring to, concerning the conviction of sin by the Holy Spirit, has been happening since Jesus died on the cross.

And to this day, which ushered in the coming of the Holy Spirit, the Holy Spirit will be that still small voice that you hear, saying "Don't do that; it is wrong." Or "Do this, it will benefit you; do it this way, it will make your life better."

John 16:9, Amplified Bible Version, Jesus is trying to tell the disciples that the Holy Spirit must come. Because people do not know or understand about sin or about righteousness, which is being in right standing with God, the Holy Spirit will come and teach us about these things, if we will let Him. People today still will not accept the statement from God's word that says He has made us be His righteousness, or that we are a righteous people, which simply means we are in right standing with God. 1 Thessalonians 5:23, (Amplified Bible), God also wants you to be kept from profane things, keeping you pure and holy in His sight, blameless until the coming of our Lord Jesus Christ. The sure way to keep yourself walking in the Love and adoration of the Lord is to daily renew your mind and life in Christ. We can do this by continuing to study God's word each and every day. I have always continued to strive to have an intimate walk with my Lord and Savior. In doing this I have a ritual that I like to do.

I study God's word. Then I play my favorite praise and worship music. While my music is playing, I pray, talking to God about things that I need help with or healing. Remember don't do all the talking, listen once in a while. Let God answer you. You will be surprised how often the Holy Spirit will speak into your spirit. And don't just ask for things; praise Him. That is what we are here on earth to do. When you are praying, and you sense the Holy Spirit moving in you, don't be afraid to open your mouth and let the spirit speak through you in that heavenly language. He tells us if we believe in Him, He will give us the desires of our hearts.

All things are possible to him who believes. If He has promised it, and you can believe it, you can have it. Are you a believer? Then all things are possible to those who believe. AMEN.

Rev. Bruce Pero

CHAPTER 8
Importance of the Name Jesus

Jesus is Peace, my Councilor, my friend, He is Love.

Let me ask this question of you, an ever-stirring question in my spirit. What is the Importance of the Name of Jesus in your life today or does it hold any significance at all? Has it been so long since you heard the name of Jesus that it holds no meaning in your life? Let's go into God's word and see how important Jesus' name really is or should be to us in our lives today. The name Jesus is derived from the Hebrew word Yeshua meaning "to deliver; to rescue," and also "God with us."

As you read on you will see exactly why God sent Jesus into this world. Acts 7:48-50 However, the Highest [the One infinitely exalted above humanity] does not dwell in houses made by human hands as the prophet [Isaiah] says. This scripture is referring to Jesus having an intimate relationship with you and me, also the fact that He dwells in us; we are Jesus' temple.

49 'Heaven is My throne, And the earth is the footstool for My feet; What kind of house will you build for Me?' says the Lord, 'Or what place is there for My rest?

50 'Was it not My hand that made all these things?'

There is a promise in John 14: 23 Jesus answered, "If a person [really] loves Me, he will keep My word [obey My teaching]; and My Father will love him, and We will come to him and make Our home (abode, special dwelling place) with him." The name of Jesus is eternal life or eternal death, depending on if we chose to believe or not believe.

Romans 14: 11 "For it is written, As I live, saith the Lord, every knee shall bow to me, and every tongue shall confess to God." 12 So then every one of us shall give an account of himself to God.

13 Let us not, therefore, judge one another anymore: but judge this rather, that no man put a stumbling block or an occasion to fall in his brother's way.

These scriptures are telling us that Jesus is our Lord and Savior. When we reach Heaven, everyone will kneel and pronounce that Jesus is our Lord and Savior. We need to remember we will only give an account of our own lives, no one else life. With that in mind, we have no right to pass judgment on anything or anyone because we are not to judge as it tells us in verse 13. Also, be careful in what we do or say about our brothers or sisters, so we will not cause them to stumble, which means falling away from following Jesus and missing going to Heaven.

Isaiah 9:6 --For to us a child is born, to us, a son is given, and the government will be on his shoulders. And he will be called Wonderful Counselor, Mighty God, Everlasting Father, and Prince of Peace.

John 3:16 -- "For God so loved the world that he gave his one and only Son, that whoever believes in him shall not perish but have eternal life.

Ephesians 6:23-- "Peace be to the brethren, and love joined with faith, from God the Father and the Lord Jesus Christ.

2 Peter 1:2-- "Grace and peace be multiplied unto you through the knowledge of God, and of Jesus our Lord.

Philippians 4:7-- "And the peace of God, which passes all understanding, shall keep your hearts and minds through Christ Jesus.

Jesus is our soon-coming King.

You see, throughout God's word there are countless scriptures to show why we should put such importance on the Name of Jesus. After all, Jesus put great importance on each and every life on this earth. Amen!

Galatians 4:6 And because you [really] are [His] sons, God has sent the [Holy] Spirit of His Son into our hearts, crying, Abba (Father)!

Revelation 19:16-On his robe and on his thigh, he has this name written: KING OF KINGS AND LORD OF LORDS.

Revelation 22:13, 16-- I am the Alpha and the Omega, the First and the Last, the Beginning and the End.

Jesus is my Savior and LORD.

Matthew 1:21 -- "She will give birth to a son, and you are to give him the name Jesus because he will save his people from their sins."

John 1:29 -The next day John saw Jesus coming toward him and said, "Look, the Lamb of God, who takes away the sin of the world!"

John 3:17 -For God did not send his Son into the world to condemn the world, but to save the world through him.

Jesus is my Healer

Psalms 107:20 He sent His word, and healed them, and delivered them from their destruction.

Matthew 15:28

Then answering, Jesus said to her, 'O woman, great is thy faith, let it be to thee as thou wilt;' and her daughter was healed from that hour.

Matthew 8:13

Then to the centurion, Jesus said, "Go; let it be done for you as you have believed." And the servant was healed at that very moment.

Isaiah 53:5

But he was wounded for our transgressions; he was bruised for our iniquities; upon him was the chastisement that brought us peace, and with his stripes, we are healed.

In closing, we can say Jesus is my peace because he gives us peace beyond all understanding. He is my counselor; one I can go to when I need help to make decisions in my life.

My closest friend that I can always rely on, my Savior, and Lord. Jesus is my Healer, and Jesus is my soon-coming King.

We should always remember, as the children's chorus says, Jesus, loves me this I know for the Bible tells me so. Amen.

Bruce Pero
11/12/2010

CHAPTER 9
Strike The Rock

On January 29TH. 2006, I was awakened from a deep sleep; it was as if someone called out to me. As I lay in my bed this message continued to go through my head, Strike the Rock, I Dare You. I felt like the Lord was sitting next to my bed telling me to strike the rock, over and over again. I said Lord what does this mean? I don't understand, then the Lord said it's just like I instructed Moses in Exodus 17:1-7. King James Version 17:1 And all the congregation of the children of Israel journeyed from the wilderness of Sin, after their journeys, according to the commandment of the Lord, and pitched in Rephidim: And there was no water for the people to drink.

2 Wherefore the people did chide with Moses, and said, "Give us water that we may drink." And Moses said unto them, "Why chide ye with me? Wherefore do ye tempt the Lord? "

3 And the people thirsted there for water; and the people murmured against Moses, and said, "Wherefore is this that

thou hast brought us up out of Egypt, to kill us and our children and our cattle with thirst?" 4 And Moses cried unto the Lord, saying, "What shall I do unto this people? they are almost ready to stone me."

5 And the Lord said unto Moses, "Go on before the people, and take with thee of the elders of Israel; and thy rod, wherewith thou smote the river, take in thine hand, and go. 6 Behold, I will stand before thee there upon the rock in Horeb; and thou shalt smite the rock, and there shall come water out of it, that the people may drink." And Moses did so in the sight of the elders of Israel.

7 And he called the name of the place Massah, and Meribah, because of the chiding of the children of Israel, and because they tempted the Lord, saying, "Is the Lord among us, or not?"

You know I have to admit when I started serving the Lord again, coming back to Lake View to attend church was the last thing on my mind. There were so many bad memories, hurt feelings, and opinions about this place that it was the last church I wanted to be a part of. But God had other plans. So little by little hurts were healed, and thoughts about what people were going to think of me, quickly fell by the wayside. Then in its place, God birthed a love in me for the people and to see things happen in His church. So many of us have had hurts, and things said to us, about us that cut to the quick. But if we don't forgive and forget, it is like drinking poison and expecting the person you have difficulties with to die. We know that doesn't work. Remember that God said He puts our sins and transgressions into the deepest part of the sea, never to be remembered again.

Micah 7:19 He shall again have compassion on us; He will subdue and tread underfoot our wickedness [destroying sin's power]. Yes, you will cast all our sins into the depths of the sea.

So just as the Bible tells us in Exodus 17:1, all the congregation of Israel moved on from the wilderness of sin in stages, according to the commandment of the Lord. Why do you think they were out there? After all, they were God's chosen people; despite their disobedience and murmuring and complaining. Sounded familiar? It should. We have all done it at one time or another. But God's Grace and Mercy are renewed each day, so good, the word tells us it is renewed every morning. Through all the turmoil that we cause, when the storms of life drag us down and we're ready to throw in the towel, remember, He still loves us and wants us to be His children.

So, when the Israelites came from the wilderness and camped at Rephidim, they found there was no water, and they were ready to stone Moses. In Exodus 17:4-6 Moses cried to the Lord. "What shall I do? These people are ready to stone me!"

Then the Lord said to Moses, "Pass on before the people and take with you some of the elders of Israel and take in your hand the rod with which you smote the Nile and go." Now if the Lord told me to take that same rod that was used on the Nile and to part the sea, I would be thinking something big is about to happen. Then the Lord told Moses to strike the rock at Horeb, and you shall have water for your people.

Now you're saying that was good. You just told us how Moses got water for the Israelites in the wilderness. You are right but also God has a message in it for you. Now it's your turn: Strike the Rock, I Dare You, you see just like the children of Israel that wandered in the wilderness of sin and came out the other side, so have we come out the other side. Some of us have lived our own life, living the way we wanted to live, trying to make it on our own. Now it is time to give God control of our lives and let Him direct our steps. Some will say, but I have been a Christian all my life, yes and that's good but have you given God control to guide your life? God is saying, just like He said to Moses, strike the rock and see that I am still with you, and the river of increase, abundance, and growth will be multiplied through your community. Strike the rock through prayer, fasting, and waiting on the Lord, for your children and grandchildren, your whole family, and see how God will work on their behalf.

God has put a desire in my heart to see His church grow, but the time is short and that is why He has said Strike the Rock Now, I Dare You, and see what I will do. Luke 10:2 He was saying to them, "The harvest is abundant [for there are many who need to hear the good news about salvation], but the workers [those available to proclaim the message of salvation] are few. Therefore, [prayerfully] ask the Lord of the harvest to send out workers into His harvest.

Perhaps you're saying what can I do? As I have taught over the years, I tell everyone, when your feet hit the floor each day, ask God to bring someone across your path so that you can share the gospel. Not only will He answer your prayer, but He will, through the Holy Spirit give you the words to say. Believe me when I say this is true because I have experienced it in my own life. There is no greater satisfaction in life than to lead a brother or sister to the Lord; to see the change in their countenance, the peace that comes over their face is priceless. So again, let me challenge all of you, strike the rock in people's lives and see our Heavenly Father change them and love them. You will be blessed for your efforts.

Amen.
Bruce Pero

♡

CHAPTER 10
We Are Called to Praise God

Through the ages of time, from Genesis to Revelations we have been called and created to praise and worship our Heavenly Father.

The word tells us to come before Him with rejoicing and thanksgiving in our hearts, making a joyful noise unto the Lord.

Genesis 4:26 To Seth, also, a son was born, whom he named Enosh (mortal man, mankind). At that [same] time men began to call on the name of the Lord [in worship through prayer, praise, and thanksgiving]. A Psalm of Praise. 150 Praise the Lord!

Praise God in His sanctuary.

Praise Him in His mighty heavens.

2 Praise Him for His mighty acts.

Praise Him according to [the abundance of] His greatness.

3 Praise Him with trumpet sound; Praise Him with harp and lyre. 4Praise Him with tambourine and dancing; Praise Him with stringed instruments and flute.

5 Praise Him with resounding cymbals; Praise Him with loud cymbals.

6 Let everything that has breath and every breath of life praise the Lord! Praise the Lord! (Hallelujah!)

We have heard every excuse in the book as to why people can't, don't, or won't worship. The Music is too loud, too fast, too slow, too old, too new, I don't know the song. It is not my style of music. The Lord said, "If my people will not worship me then the very rocks will cry out in worship." Luke 19:39-40 Some of the Pharisees from the crowd said to Him, "Teacher, rebuke Your disciples [for shouting these Messianic praises]."

40 Jesus replied, "I tell you, if these [people] keep silent, the stones will cry out [in praise]!"

I would hate to think we would be replaced by a bunch of rocks. That the ground we stand on would worship our God because we do not have the drive or fortitude to worship the One that died for us? the one that gave His life so that I could live with the knowledge that I was set free from any guilt or condemnation. So, after witnessing the lack of worship in our churches over the years, I started to ask some very important questions. I could not believe that this was transpiring before my eyes. As the worship songs were being played, people would stand with hands in their pockets, looking around as if asking will this ever be over. Others felt it was a perfect time to discuss where to go for lunch after the service. Then we have some that feel it's just as easy to sit and mouth the words to How Great Though Art, rather than stand and really sing it and let the Lord know you really feel and think He is as

Great as the words say. I first prayed and asked My Heavenly Father to forgive me for even being a part of such a thing.

If we can't praise our Heavenly Father here on earth and do it with all the enthusiasm and gusto we can muster, how are we to praise our Lord around the throne of God? The Throne and Worship of the Creator Revelation 4:5-11 "From the throne came flashes of lightning and [rumbling] sounds and peals of thunder. Seven lamps of fire were burning in front of the throne, which are the seven Spirits of God.

6 and in front of the throne there was something like a sea or large expanse of glass, like [the clearest] crystal. In the center and around the throne were four living creatures who were full of eyes in front and behind [seeing everything and knowing everything that is around them].

7 The first living creature was like a lion, the second creature was like a calf (ox), the third creature had the face of a man, and the fourth creature was like a flying eagle.

8 And the four living creatures, each one of them having six wings, are full of eyes all over and within [underneath their wings]; and day and night they never stop saying,

"Holy, holy, holy [is the] Lord God, the Almighty [the Omnipotent, the Ruler of all], who was and who is and who is to come [the unchanging, eternal God]."

9 Whenever the living creatures give glory and honor and thanksgiving to Him who sits on the throne, to Him who lives forever and ever, 10 the twenty-four elders fall down before Him who sits on the throne, and they worship Him who lives forever and ever; and they throw down their crowns before the throne, saying,

11 "Worthy are You, our Lord and God, to receive the glory and the honor and the power; for You created all things, and because of Your will they exist and were created and brought into being."

Then I asked Him, how can we change this and get the worship back where it should be? Then I felt the Lord leading me to do a teaching on the following words. Thanksgiving, we are to give thanks to our Lord and Saviour for our very existence. We are to thank Him for all He provides for us. Psalm 37:25 "I have been young, and now am old; yet have I not seen the righteous forsaken, nor his seed begging bread. Praise," Psalm 150:6 "Let everything that has breath and every breath of life praise the Lord!" Praise the Lord! (Hallelujah!) Glorifying, Galatians 1:24 And they were glorifying God [as the Author and Source of what had taken place and all that had been accomplished] in me. I can say this as well, for the changes in my life since Christ became my Lord and Savior, I give Glory to my Lord and King of Kings. And to sum it up I say Hallelujah, I Rejoice at the mention of His name. AMEN. So, people of God's church I implore you to worship Him with all your hearts. This is just a dress rehearsal for Heaven to come. Amen!!!

June 6TH 2011
C. Bruce Pero

CHAPTER 11
Does God Know Me?

·This is a message for all who are thinking is God real, does God really care about me, does He even know me? Matthew 10:30 Amplified Bible, "but even the very hairs of your head are all numbered" [for the father is sovereign and has complete knowledge].

The answer to the question, does God know me, is a resounding Yes, God loves and cares about you more than you can ever imagine. The scriptures He gave me this morning have been so real in my life, I know if you read them over and truly study them you will find He loves you also. The title alone is powerful.

The words from David, (The Prayer of a Believing Heart.) to our Heavenly Father. Psalm 139

1 "O Lord, you have searched me [thoroughly] and have known me. 2 You know my down-sitting and my uprising; You understand my thought afar off. 3 You sift and search out my path and my lying down, and You are acquainted with all my ways.

4 For there is not a word in my tongue [still UN-uttered], but behold, O Lord, you know it altogether.

5 You have beset me and shut me in—behind and before, and You have laid Your hand upon me.

6 Your [infinite] knowledge is too wonderful for me; it is high above me, and I cannot reach it.

7 Where could I go from Your Spirit? Or where could I flee from Your presence?

8 If I ascend up into heaven, you are there; if I make my bed in Hell (the place of the dead), behold, you are there.

9 If I take the wings of the morning or dwell in the uttermost parts of the sea,

10 Even there shall Your hand lead me, and your right hand shall hold me."

When David pends these words, he knew such a presence of God through the Holy Spirit in his life that regardless of where he was or what he was going through, God was always with him.

If we continually study these scriptures, we will find out as David did that there is not one thing that our heavenly Father does not know about you and me. See what God's word tells us in this next scripture This is David again speaking about our Lord. 12 "Even the darkness is not dark to You and conceals nothing from You, But the night shines as bright as the day; Darkness and light are alike to You.

13 You made all the delicate, inner parts of my body and knit them together in my mother's womb.14 Thank you for making me so wonderfully complex! It is amazing to think about. Your workmanship is marvelous—and how well I

know it. 15 You were there while I was being formed in utter seclusion! 16 You saw me before I was born and scheduled each day of my life before I began to breathe. Every day was recorded in your book!"

Think about it. Every day of your life is recorded in the books in Heaven. God knows us so well that the word says it pleased Him to make us the Gentiles part of His family. Ephesians 1:5 "Having predesignated us unto the adoption of children by Jesus Christ to Himself, according to the good pleasure of His will.

To sum it up, does God know me, does God really care about me, and does God love me? In this next scripture found in John 14:23, Jesus answered and said unto him, "If a man loves me, he will keep my words: and my Father will love him, and we will come unto him, and make our abode with him." Amen!!!

It has been said, there is nothing you can do to make God love you anymore. Also, there is nothing you can do to make Him love you any less. So, what are you waiting for accept Him as your Lord and Savior and let Him show you how much He loves you and cares for you. It will be a choice you will never regret.

Blessings
Rev Bruce Pero

CHAPTER 12
Heart Felt words

You know there is a phrase that comes up on my home page on Facebook every day. It goes like this, (what's on your mind)?

It is actually a very interesting question because it opens up the opportunity for one to go in so many diverse directions.

Some of the pleasantries about family and friends, others about concerns in our community. But in the last year, people have taken on a spirit of the fear of the unknown, and even allowed it to fester into anger against one another. God's word very clearly states in 2 Timothy 1;7 "For God hath not given us the spirit of fear, but of power, and of love, and of a sound mind."

The very idea is that people could be drawn into a spirit of intimidation, fear, and manipulation, not to mention control, which to me is very sad. People who were once close friends now won't even look at one another. Families have fallen into disarray, all for what we think is a good reason, because someone said, I'm right you're wrong; you don't care about others; you just care about yourself, more sadness!

Psalm 133 "Behold, how good and how pleasant it is for brethren to dwell together in unity!" We are to be united as one, we are to love one another as Jesus has instructed us. John 13:34 I am giving you a new commandment, that you love one another. Just as I have loved you, so you too are to love one another.

Ephesians 2:14 "For He is [Himself] our peace (our bond of unity and harmony). He has made us both [Jew and Gentile] one [body], and has broken down (destroyed, abolished) the hostile dividing wall between us."

I have my own theory about this dilemma.

It goes like this. It seems that the powers that be would rather see people in turmoil and in fear because it is easier to control them when they are fearful and confused.

God's word tells us very clearly this is not the case, as we read in,

1 Peter 5:8 Be sober [well balanced and self-disciplined], be alert and cautious at all times. "That enemy of yours, the devil, prowls around like a roaring lion [fiercely hungry], seeking someone to devour".

This verse clearly explains who and what the plan has been from the beginning; to destroy the unity of the believers and the church.

Then there is the reality that some people stand to gain financially from the position our country has been thrown into, to our shame!

My Lord put me into this world for a reason and whether I go out with covid or a car wreck I have work to do for my Lord.

This word was revealed to me when the pandemic started.

In these last few days, God has brought it back to my memory.

The Lord would say, take your focus off the things taking place in this world; Put it back on your God as He is about shaking the world in these last days to do a new thing.

Isaiah 24:13 New living translation. 13 throughout the earth the story is the same only a remnant is left, like the stray olives left on the tree or the few grapes left on the vine after harvest.

Hebrews 12:26-29 New Living Translation. 26 When God spoke from mount Sinai His voice shook the earth, but now he makes another promise: "once again I will shake not only the earth but the heavens also," 27 This means all of creation will be shaken and removed so that only unshakable things will remain. 28 Since we are receiving a Kingdom that is unshakable, let us be thankful and please God by worshiping Him with holy fear and awe.

29 For our God is a devouring fire.

This is not a license to twist and manipulate the world for your own financial and political gain.

Psalm 133:1 "Behold, how good and how pleasant it is for brethren to dwell together in unity!" As the body of Christ, and also as His church, we must work in unity, which means in all areas of our lives. So, I'll sum it up this way; as an old song says, "I'm a winner either way if I go or if I stay."

So, until that time comes, let me encourage everyone that reads this, to try to live in unity, show love to each other, be kind to those less fortunate and remember, Jesus, Loves you.

Blessings
Rev Bruce Pero

♡

CHAPTER 13
Love

I asked the Lord what He wanted me to share with you and I immediately heard, "Tell them I love them". Wow! So, I went to the Scriptures and began reading the many places where we are told about God's love for us. The first place I went looking for Scriptures on Love, was in 1 John Chapter 4. Verse 8 tells us that God is love. Then in verse 9, we are told that God showed how much He loved us by sending Jesus into the world so that we could live through Him. Without Jesus, we have no life at all. Verse 10 tells us that the love we are talking about here is the great love that God had for us.... not the love that we have for God. There is a big difference. Our love, or what we think is love, cannot even compare to God's love. It says here that God loved us so much that He sent Jesus to be the sacrifice for our sins.

(John 3:16) "For God so [greatly] loved and dearly prized the world, that He [even] gave His [One and] [a]only begotten Son so that whoever believes and trusts in Him [as Savior] shall not perish but have eternal life."

Romans 5:8 echoes this, "But God clearly shows and proves His own love for us, by the fact that while we were still sinners, Christ died for us." God demonstrates his love for us in these scriptures and by His actions, we can now know God's heart. "While we were still sinners, Christ died for us." (Also, Ephesians 2:4,5 4 "But God, who is rich in mercy, for His great love wherewith he loved us.

5 Even when we were dead in sins He hath quickened us together with Christ, (by grace ye are saved;)) When we were still sinners...God sent Jesus to die for us."

That's an amazing love!! We know these Scriptures; we have heard them so many times......but do we really get them? How great is God's love for us? Can we even begin to fathom it? I asked this question, and the Lord led me to more Scriptures.

Romans 8:29-39, 29 "For those God foreknew he also predestined to be conformed to the likeness of his Son, that he might be the firstborn among many brothers." God knew every person before they ever came to this earth!!!

That's you and me....and everyone who has ever lived, and everyone who ever will live in the future. And... it's His plan that each one of us become like Jesus!! That means VICTORY!!! God loves us so much that He designed and planned for us to live in victory...not in defeat, but victory! That is God's, great love!

30 "And those He predestined, He also called; those He called, He also justified; those He justified, he also glorified." Wow! God has done all of these things for us!! 1. Predestined -in this verse this means that He per-planned for us to be like

Jesus 2. Called -to a specific purpose -God has a special plan for each one of us that is unique.

3. Justified -freed, made innocent -just-as if-I'd-never sinned -God did this for ALL! 4. Glorified -made us glorious (caused us to be treated much better than would normally be considered) So, He treats us much better than we deserve.... or what we think we deserve. He chooses to see us this way and treats us this way!!!! Wow!! God's love includes all this! He has chosen each one of us especially for completing part of His grand master plan......and He has made us able to do it by removing the hindrances of unworthiness, shame, and inadequacies. He sees us and treats us just like Jesus!!! That's great love!!

31 "What, then, shall we say in response to this? If God is for us, who can be against us?"

(We must understand that God's love is so great for us that there is nothing or no one who can be against us.

Oh, it may look like things or people are against us, but in reality.... the reality of the Word....of LOVE....of God and His way....in this reality...which is the real thing... NOTHING can be against us!!

32 "He who did not spare his own Son, but gave Him up for us all—how will he not also, along with Him, graciously give us all things?" God gave us His Son, Jesus. Will He not give us everything else, too? Jesus was the greatest gift.... everything else is just "pocket change"!! (Simple or easy to give) 33 "Who will bring any charge against those whom God has chosen?"

It is God who justifies. Once we have received what God has done for us, can anyone accuse us? Who is the accuser of the brethren? (Satan) Revelation 12:10, 11 "And I heard a loud voice saying in heaven, Now is come salvation, and strength, and the kingdom of our God, and the power of his Christ: for the accuser of our brethren is cast down, which accused them before our God day and night. 11 And they overcame him by the blood of the Lamb, and by the word of their testimony, and they loved not their lives unto the death."

Satan has been accusing the children of God, trying to dispense his hate for a long time, but the children of God have been overcoming these accusations by the blood of the Lamb and the word of their testimony!!! Hallelujah! This means that Satan can accuse us, but he cannot be victorious over us with his actions. We can use the blood of Jesus against him and the word of God against him. We can tell Satan that he is defeated because of what Jesus accomplished on the cross. We can use the Scriptures....just like Jesus did in Matthew 4 to get rid of this accuser.

Do you understand what I am saying??? Yes, there is an accuser, but he is just blowing hot air.

His words are meaningless if we are under the wings of God.

If we have received forgiveness, there is nothing that we can be accused of!!! It's already under the blood! The price has been paid and we are free!!! Glory to God! 34 "Who is he that condemns? Christ Jesus, who died—more than that, who was raised to life—is at the right hand of God and is also interceding for us."

Again, Satan is the condemner, but he cannot condemn us of what we are forgiven of. Hallelujah!!

Romans 8:1 "There is therefore now no condemnation to them which are in Christ Jesus, who walk not after the flesh, but after the Spirit. 35 Who shall separate us from the love of Christ? Shall trouble or hardship or persecution or famine or nakedness or danger or sword? 36 As it is written: "For your sake, we face death all day long; we are considered as sheep to be slaughtered."

37No, in all these things we are more than conquerors through him who loved us. Because of God's great love for us, we have been made victorious!" This verse says that we are MORE than conquerors through Christ. That, my friends, is good news!!!! Amen!!! How can we be more than a conqueror????? The conquering (or fighting and winning) has already been done.... we live in victory!! The battle is won! Paul goes on...

38 "For I am convinced that neither death nor life, neither angels nor demons, neither the present nor the future, nor any powers, 39neither height nor depth, nor anything else in all creation, will be able to separate us from the love of God that is in Christ Jesus our Lord." Paul knew God intimately and we as believers can have that same intimate walk with our Lord, Paul was so convinced that absolutely nothing could separate us from God's love. This means that God's love for us...keeps us always together with Him. The Bible says that He never leaves us or forsakes us... He's not going to abandon us.... ever! God's love is with us ALWAYS, FOREVER!!!

We can't run away from it or escape it, no matter what!!! Are you getting the picture of how much God really loves you?

Are you beginning to understand the greatness and over-whelmingly hugeness of His love for ALL people? We really need to meditate and think about this. We need to go to the Scriptures and do a study on "LOVE". We will be deeply moved when we do!! So, what do we do with this informa-tion? 1. We receive comfort in knowing that we are loved... that's one thing. Take that same Love out into the world and share it, letting others experience God's love.

Many people feel unloved, but how can we possibly feel unloved when we have just seen how much God loves us??? So, whenever you are getting these thoughts or feelings of not being loved, remind yourself how much God loves you and thank Him for loving you so much. I guarantee those undesirable thoughts and feelings will disappear. Knowing that we are loved gives us confidence. When we are confi-dent, we can do whatever our Lord wants us to do.

There is one more thing that I sense to mention to you today. As I was reading through the Scriptures about love, I kept hearing the same thing over and over again. What I heard were words of instruction. It seems that God has shown us how much He loves us as an example for us to live by. It's a tall order to live up to, but over and over again, I read it, you can do your own study and read it for yourself, too! The words of instruction were, "Love one another!" The Lord wants us to live in victory. We read this in Romans Chapter 8. How can we do it?

Romans 5:5 "And hope make us not ashamed; because the love of God is shed abroad in our hearts by the Holy Ghost which is given unto us." This same love that God loves us with, has been given to us. That's really hard to imagine, but the Bible says that it's true!! We need to spend some time thinking about this and getting into the picture we have of ourselves.

If God's love is in us, then we must be able to love as He loves. Selah! He then tells us in numerous places that that is His desire for us.

1 John 4:11 Beloved, if God so loved us, we ought also to love one another. Eph. 5:2 "And walk in love, as Christ also hath loved us, and hath given Himself for us an offering and a sacrifice to God for a sweet-smelling savor. John 13:34, 35, A new commandment I give unto you, that ye love one another; as I have loved you, that ye also love one another. 35 By this shall all men know that ye are my disciples if ye have love one to another."

So, we can see here that there is something that God wants us to do with His love. Once we have received it, we are to give it out and walk in it...DO IT!!! James 1:22 tells us to be doers of the word Matthew 10:8 tells us to freely give what we have freely received. God freely gave us Jesus to show us the love of the Father and Jesus freely gave Himself so that we could receive that same love, and in turn, give it away to others. The Bible tells us who we are supposed to love with this love we have received.

Let me conclude with this section of Scripture... Matthew 5:43-48 43"You have heard that it was said, 'Love your neighbor and hate your enemy.' 44 But I tell you: Love your enemies and pray for those who persecute you, 45 That you may be sons of your Father in heaven. He causes his sun to rise on the evil and the good and sends rain on the righteous and the unrighteous. 46 If you love those who love you, what reward will you get? Are not even the tax collectors doing that? 47 And if you greet only your brothers, what are you doing more than others? Do not even pagans do that?

48 Be perfect, therefore, as your heavenly Father is perfect." The word "perfect" here means complete in mental and moral character. So, we are being taught about the character of God here.

This is one more way that we can be conformed to the image of Christ as we read about at the beginning. God is letting us in on a secret to success here. Love is a major part of our Christian lives and is the key to our success. There are so many more things I would like to say about this, but for now, I need to stop here.

We need to SELAH....pause and think about this......but not only pause and think, but we must also practice it in our daily lives.

We must examine our lives and see where we are not showing love...and then start loving. This is not condemnation or accusation, but this is exhortation and encouragement for you.

This is what the Lord would say to you today. James 1:22 "Be ye doers of the word and not hearers only, deceiving your own selves." This Christian walk is all about application. We learn something from the word and then we do it in our lives.

That's how we become conformed to the image of Christ. That's how people will know that we are Christians. Amen!!!!

Revised on Feb. 25,2022
Rev Bruce Pero

CHAPTER 14
Someday

Thousands of years before Jesus was called the Lamb of God, God promised forgiveness, "Someday," he promised Hosea, "Someday I will remember their sins no more,"

'Someday," God confided to Jeremiah, "these people will be my people and I will be their God." You see God already had a plan in the works for the Jewish people. What was the spiritual condition of the Gentile's world before Christ came into the picture? The Gentile people are where we came into the picture. God's word makes it very clear where we stood at this time in history.

(Amplified) Ephesians 2:12-16 (Remember) that you were at that time separated (living apart) from Christ (excluded from all parts of Him), utterly estranged and outlawed from the rights of Israel as a nation, and strangers with no share in the sacred compacts of the (Messianic) promise (with no knowledge of or rights in God's agreement, His covenants). And you had no hope (no promise); you were in the world without God.

13, "But now in Christ Jesus, you who were so far away, through the blood of Christ have been brought near.

14, "For He is (Himself) our peace (our bond of unity and harmony). He has made us both (Jew and Gentile) one (body) and has broken down (destroyed, abolished) the hostile dividing wall between us."

15 By abolishing in His (own crucified) flesh the enmity (caused by) the Law with its decrees and ordinances (which He annulled): that He from the two might create in Himself one new man (one new quality of humanity out of two), so making peace.

16 "And (He designed) to reconcile to God both (Jew and Gentile, united) in a single body by the means of His cross, thereby killing the mutual enmity and bringing the feud to an end."

Before Ephesians 2: 12-16 we should remember, God, knew us before we were formed in our mother's womb, we were predestined to be His children.

Ephesians 1:4-7 "Even as (in His love) He chose us (actually picked us out for Himself as His own) in Christ before the foundations of the world, that we should be holy (consecrated and set apart for Him) and blameless in His sight, even above reproach, before Him in love."

5, "For He foreordained us (destined us, planned in love for us) to be ADOPTED (revealed) as His own children through Jesus Christ by the purpose of His will (because it pleased Him and was His Kind intent). 6 (so that we might be) to the praise and the commendation of His glorious grace (favor and mercy), which He so freely bestowed on us in the beloved.

7 In Him we have redemption (deliverance and salvation) through His blood, the remission (forgiveness) of our sins (shortcomings and trespasses), by the riches and the generosity of His gracious favor."

"And someday," wrote David, "the mistakes of men will be tossed, {not under a rug or behind the sofa, but far, far away} as far as the east is from the west." And do you know what? That someday came, on a garbage heap outside of Jerusalem. Someday the almighty God, who has every right to make me burn forever, will look past my apathy, my gluttony, my lying, and my lusting. He will point to the cross and invite me to come...for-given...forever. Amen!!!!

Ephesians 2:19-22 "Now you who are not Jewish are not foreigners or strangers any longer but are citizens together with God's Holy people. You belong to God's family."

20, You are like a building that was built on the foundation of the apostles and prophets.

Christ Jesus Himself is the most important stone, in the building.

21 And the whole building is joined together in Christ. He made it grow and become a Holy temple in the Lord.

22 And in Christ you, too, are being built together with the Jews into a place where God lives through the Spirit.

What three things Has redemption brought to us?

In Christ, we have our redemption from Satan's dominion.

It is Eternal Redemption (this is forever)

It is operative now, (meaning the instant we accept Christ as our Lord and Savior, we become the righteousness of God.

2nd Corinthians 5:21 "For our sake He made Christ be sin Who knew no sin, that in and through Him we might become (endued with, viewed as being in, and examples of) the righteousness of God;" (what we ought to be, approved and acceptable and in right relationship with Him, by His goodness).

Revelation 1:18 "And the Ever-living One (I am, living in the eternity of the eternities). I died, but see, I am alive forevermore, and I possess the keys of death and Hades (the realm of the dead).

Jesus, who has the keys of Death and Hades is the Head and Lord of the New Creation. The Holy Spirit through the Word can make our present vital rights in redemption a reality. The days of weakness and failure are ended for the man who knows the Word and dares to act upon it.

What is the meaning of remission?

Remission means to wipe out everything we have ever done up to the time we come to Christ and to the end of the ages. No matter how much Satan has entrapped us in his snares, the minute we are Born Again we stand before God as New Creations without the smell of our past life upon our spirit.

The instant we are Born Again, we become the righteousness of God in Christ. The instant we become the righteousness of God, Satan's dominion over us is broken.

2 Corinthians 5:21 "He hath made him sin for us, who knew no sin; that we might be made the righteousness of God Himself."

Explain the secret of the New Creation truth, what is the characteristic of the New Creation?

This is not only a theological fact but a living reality.

2nd Corinthians 5:17, "Therefore, if any person is in Christ (the Messiah) he is a new creation (a new creature altogether); the old (previous moral and spiritual condition) has passed away. Behold, the fresh and new has come."

All these things are of God Who has reconciled us unto Himself.

Now note it carefully, "If any man is in Christ." When we accept Christ as our Savior and confess Him as our Lord, we become a branch of the Vine.

John 15:5 "I am the Vine; you are the Branches. Whosoever lives in Me and I in him bears much (abundant) fruit. However, apart from Me (cut off from vital union with Me), you can do nothing."

We become utterly one with Christ.

The characteristic of the new Creation is that we become partakers of His Divine Nature. 2nd Peter 1:4, Using these He has bestowed on us His precious and exceedingly great promise, so that through them you may escape (by flight) from the moral decay (rottenness and corruption) that is in the world because of the covetousness (lust greed), and become sharers (partakers) of the Divine Nature.

The escape is to Eternal Life. "Jesus said I come that they may have life and have it more abundantly." The word "Life" is from the Greek word "Zoe." It means God's Divine Nature.

1 John 5:13, "These things I have written unto you that believe in the name of the Son of God; that ye may know

that ye have eternal life and that ye may believe in the name of the Son of God." The instant you believe you possess the Father's nature.

How are we to use the Sword of the Spirit?

In 2nd Corinthians 11:3, Paul says, "But I fear, lest by any means as the serpent beguiled Eve in his craftiness, your minds might be corrupted from the purity that is in Christ." And so, He gave us the Sword of the Spirit- which is the Word of God. This sword of the spirit is NEVER used to wound or to slay men, but it is used against the Adversary; "for our combat is not against flesh and blood, but against principalities and powers, against rulers of the world's powers." You see, we have come out of the darkness into the light, out of the kingdom of Satan into the kingdom of the Son of His love, and our combat is against the forces of darkness that surround us. For we are in the light, and we walk in the light as He is in the light. That light is the Word. That light is love. That light gives us fellowship and companionship with the Father and with Jesus. You remember in 1 John 3:8 that the Spirit tells us about Jesus: "To the end was the Son of God manifested, that He might destroy the works of the Devil. What other great weapon has the father given us to use to combat the powers of darkness? Read in Ephesians 6:13-20,

13, "Therefore put on God's complete armor, that you may be able to resist and stand your ground on an evil day (of danger), and, having done all (the crisis demands), to stand (firmly in your place)."

14 "Stand, therefore (hold your ground), having tightened the belt of truth around your loins and having put on

the breastplate of integrity and of moral rectitude and right standing with God."

15 "And having shod your feet in preparation (to face the enemy with the firm-footed stability, the promptness, and the readiness produced by the good news) of the gospel."

16 "Lift up over all the (covering) shield of saving faith, upon which you can quench all the flaming missiles of the wicked (one)."

17. "And take the helmet of salvation and the Sword that the Spirit wields, which is the Word of God."

18 "Pray at all times (on every occasion, in every season) in the spirit, with all (manner of) prayer and entreaty. To that end keep alert and watch with strong purpose and perseverance, interceding on behalf of all the saints (God's consecrated people."

Paul writes I ask that you take verses 19 and 20, personally for me and all your brothers and sisters in Christ.

19 "And (PRAY) also for me, that (freedom of) utterance may be given me, that I may open my mouth to proclaim boldly the mystery of the good news (the Gospel)."

20. "For which I am an ambassador in a coupling chain (in prison. Pray) that I may declare it boldly and courageously, as I ought to do." AMEN.

Rev Bruce Pero

CHAPTER 15
Redeemed

To show how much God loves us and to show the progression of our redemption, and the actual status of our relationship with Jesus 1 Corinthians 8:6 Amplified Bible 6 says, " Yet for us there is but one God, the Father, who is the source of all things, and we exist for Him; and one Lord, Jesus Christ, by whom are all things [that have been created], and we [believers exist and have life and have been redeemed] through Him."

At first, we were called His sheep. You see this when Jesus was talking to Peter at the last supper.

John 10:27, Jesus says, "The sheep that are My own hear me and are listening to My voice, and I know them, and they follow Me."

Then He progressed, calling us "... the servants of our Heavenly Father." 1 Corinthians 4:1 says, "So then, let us [apostles] be looked upon as ministering Servants of Christ and stewards (trustees) of the mysteries (the secret purposes) of God."

Then we move closer to God into His Family status. Not only did God adopt us as His children, so we can have a closer intimacy "with" God. We graduate as His sons and daughters. Many times, as God's children we tend to go down other paths that God never intended for us to go; paths that quite often lead us into troubled waters. But as our Heavenly Father, He is always there to put us back on the right path.

One thing I've always said, we can run from God and his plan for our lives, but God will never take His hand off of our lives He is always there for us to steer us in the right direction. We only have to listen to that still small voice and obey what He is directing us to do.

Psalms 107:2" Let the redeemed of the Lord say so, Whom He has redeemed from the hand of the adversary.

2 Corinthians 6:18 "And I will be a Father to you, and you shall be My sons and daughters, says the Lord Almighty".

God's word tells us in, Ephesians 1:5 "For He foreordained us (destined us, planned in love for us) to be adopted (revealed) as His own children through Jesus Christ, by the purpose of His will." [because it pleased Him and was His kind intent]—

Isaiah 46:3,4 says, "I have created you and cared for you since you were born. 4 I will be your God through all your lifetime. Yes, even when your hair is white with age, I made you and I will care for you. I will carry you along and be your Savior."

Not only did God adopt us as His children, but He called us His sons and daughters. It has often been said that there is nothing you can do to make God love you any less. But remember there is nothing you can do to make Him love you anymore. God's love for you is a never-ending love. The final step of the progression of our relationship with the Lord is when we are in love with our Lord and Savior. This takes place at the Marriage Super of the Lamb.

Revelation 19:7 "Let us rejoice and shout for joy [exulting and triumphant]! Let us celebrate and ascribe to Him glory and honor, for the marriage of the Lamb [Jesus][at last] has come, and His bride has prepared herself."

Revelation 19:8-9 Amplified Bible 8 "She has been permitted to dress in fine linen, dazzling white and clean—for the fine linen signifies the righteous acts of the saints [the ethical conduct, personal integrity, moral courage, and godly character of believers"].9 Then the angel said to me, "Write, 'Blessed are those who are invited to the marriage supper of the Lamb." And he said to me [further], "These are the true and exact words of God."

The way to prepare ourselves for this day is to accept Jesus Christ into our lives as our Lord and Savior, Jesus said, "All that call on my name will be saved." Remember the thief on the cross.

Luke 23:43 And Jesus said unto him, "Verily I say unto thee, today shalt thou be with me in paradise."

Acts 2:21 "And it shall come to pass, that whosoever shall call on the name of the Lord shall be saved." So, I encourage you to have an intimate walk with God by studying His word daily and also spending time talking to Him. The Bible says to come boldly into the throne room of God, come and let God know what is on your heart. Hebrews 4:16 Let us, therefore, come boldly unto the throne of grace, that we may obtain mercy, and find grace to help in time of need. Remember His word. He will give you the desires of your heart that you need. So, try Jesus today, what do you have to lose? Amen.

Rev. Bruce Pero

CHAPTER 16
The End-Time Plan

The media world and a few others would like us to believe that COVID-19 is the worst thing we ever had to deal with. But what about vaccinating seven billion people with a vaccine that could kill a third of the people that get it. A vaccine that has never been FDA approved. Who wants to be first? Then our Governments will say, we'll chip you so you won't have to carry any Id and all your personal records will be on hand for the government. Also, through this tracking device, the government will know exactly where you are and who you're coming in contact with; remember we have to be good little sheep and stay in step and in line. This gets better! Just wait till the digital currency they're working on gets in place. We won't have to carry that dirty, old money around anymore, we just go online to see how much is in our accounts;' the same as our government will be able to do. We get to spend it using that cool tracking chip they put in your hand because it will have all your banking info on it as well. You know this is sounding more and more, like a one-world order, possibly, even a -World Dictatorship. Perhaps some of the elites could help us with this but remember there are only a few of the toads in the puddle. One thing I almost forgot! Those familiar with Bible Prophecy and apocalyptic end-time events have a name for this period. These are the people that have made a commitment and accepted a personal relationship with Jesus Christ as Lord and Savior.

These are those that are ready for the rapture or as God's word says the great "catching away." They will not be around for these days. Then the Great Tribulation will take place for seven years, halfway through at three and one half years.

The Anti Christ will usher in the Mark of the Beast as recorded in Revelation 13...no one can buy or sell without the mark containing all our personal ID as well, as our free pass straight to hell if we take the mark. If you refuse the mark you will have your head cut off as punishment for refusing to take the mark as a follower of the Anti Christ. Also, the Bible talks about plagues, diseases, and sicknesses like we have never seen before dumped on our world.

Luke 21:25-27 King James Version 25 "And there shall be signs in the sun, and in the moon, and in the stars; and upon the earth distress of nations, with perplexity; the sea and the waves roaring.

26 Men's hearts failing them for fear, and for looking after those things which are coming on the earth: for the powers of heaven shall be shaken. 27 And then shall they see the son of man coming in a cloud with power and great glory." If you don't believe me read Daniel 12, Mark 13, Revelation 13. 2 Timothy 1:7 "For God hath not given us the spirit of fear; but

of power, and of love, and of a sound mind." But there are so many things that will take place before all this happens. What is being talked about in these scriptures are referring to the seven years of the tribulation, which you can also read about in the scripture references that are given previously.

2 Timothy 3:1-3 But mark this: "There will be terrible times in the last days. 2 People will be lovers of themselves, lovers of money, boastful, proud, abusive, disobedient to their parents, ungrateful, unholy,

3 without love, unforgiving, slanderous, without self-control, brutal, not lovers of the good."

2 Timothy 4:1-5 New International Version, "In the presence of God and of Christ Jesus, who will judge the living and the dead, and given his appearing and his kingdom, I give you this charge:

2 Preach the word; be prepared in season and out of season; correct, rebuke and encourage—with great patience and careful instruction.

3 For the time will come when people will not put up with sound doctrine. Instead, to suit their own desires, they will gather around them a great number of teachers (Preachers) to say what their itching ears want to hear. 4 They will turn their ears away from the truth and turn aside to myths. 5 But you, keep your head in all situations, endure hardship, do the work of an evangelist, discharge all the duties of your ministry." This very thing that is mentioned in

2 Timothy 4:1-5 is in fact in our churches today. Where board members and deacons of the churches are actually telling the preachers what to preach in their sermons, what

to say and what to stay clear of so as not to offend any of the parishioners.

This is something I never thought I would see but God's word tells us it will happen as people stray away from truly serving our Lord with a committed heart. The Bible tells how God will separate the sheep and the goats, the sheep being the followers that worship Him in spirit and truth, and the goats and wolves in sheep's clothing are the ones going through the motions of serving God.

Matthew 15:8 "This people draw near unto me with their mouth and honor me only with their lips, but their heart is far from me."

In closing, this message is not to discourage anyone, on the contrary, it is to open our eyes and hopefully prepare people for what we are actually going through and what is ahead of us. Stop listening to all the media and start looking into God's word; it will tell you what is really going on. Some will say, oh he has just become one of those religious nuts. Honestly, I and Jesus cannot stand religions or religious people, but I will love them and pray for them. My Bible tells me that the end times will be as in the days of Noah.

Matthew 24:35-42 King James Version 35 "Heaven and earth shall pass away, but my words shall not pass away. 36 But of that day and hour knoweth no man, no, not the angels of heaven, but my Father only."

37 "But as the days of Noah were, so shall also the coming of the Son of man be. 38 For as in the days that were before the flood they were eating and drinking, marrying and giving in marriage until the day that they entered into the ark, 39

And knew not until the flood came, and took them all away; so, shall also the coming of the Son of man be."

40 "Then shall two be in the field; the one shall be taken, and the other left. 41 Two women shall be grinding at the mill; the one shall be taken, and the other left. 42 Watch therefore: for ye know not what hour your Lord doth come." So, my prayer for everyone is that we find ourselves ready for Jesus' return for His church.

So, my final question is this if Jesus were to return in the next hour, do you know in your heart where you will spend eternity? Will it be Heaven or Hell? They both do exist whether we choose to believe it or not. But the Good news in the Bible says, "all that call on the name of Jesus will be saved." So today just say, Jesus, forgive me of all my sins, come into my heart. I make you Lord of my life. Amen! If you have done this, you are on your way to Heaven, and I look forward to seeing you all there. Amen!!

December 6, 2021
Rev. Bruce Pero

CHAPTER 17
My Creator, A Worthy Confidant

1. God Is Righteous
2. God Is Trustworthy
3. God Is a Refuge
4. God Is Faithful

Intimacy connotes familiarity and closeness.

It involves our deepest nature, and it is marked by a friendship developed through long association. For us to become intimate with another, we must find him a true confidant-one in whom we can safely confide our secrets.

Most of us look for someone we respect as wise and just; one we can trust implicitly; one we feel safe and secure with; one who will respond to us, help us in all ways, available whenever we want to share. True confidants are rare, and fortunate are those who have one. There is one who meets this criteria perfectly: the Keeper of souls who never sleeps, who calls us into fellowship- "Call to Me, and I will answer you, and I will tell you great and mighty things, which you do not know" (Jeremiah 33:3).

The marvelous affirmation of the psalmists is that the Creator of the vast universe is also our intimate Confidant.

1: GOD Is Righteous

"Righteousness and justice are the foundation of Your throne; Mercy and truth go before Your face.

Blessed are the people who know the joyful sound! They walk, O Lord, in the light of Your countenance."

Psalm 89:14-15 (NKJV)

Romans 5:9 "Therefore, since we are now justified (acquitted, made righteous, and brought into right relationship with God) by Christ's blood, how much more [certain is it that] we shall be saved by Him from the indignation and wrath of God."

The word in this song fits our meaning as much as anything else.

My hope is built on nothing less
Then Jesus' blood and righteousness
I dare not trust the sweetest frame,
But wholly lean on Jesus' name. Amen!

Our Father, we love Thee for Thy justice. We acknowledge that thy judgments are true and righteous altogether. Thy justice upholds the order of the universe and guarantees the safety of all who put their trust in Thee. We live because Thou art just -and merciful. Holy, Holy, Holy, Lord God Almighty,

righteous in all Thy ways and Holy in all Thy works. Amen.
By A. W. Tozer

It is comforting to know that God is righteous.
Righteousness essentially means "meeting the standard of
what is right and just." Righteousness involves goodness,
uprightness, integrity, morality, and purity. Sinclair Ferguson
expounds further by asking the question, "But what of the
righteousness of God? The idea behind the Biblical word
righteousness is probably 'conformity to a norm.' Given that
norm, righteousness is the situation in which things are what
they ought to be.

2: God is Trustworthy

In the Old Testament, righteousness is associated with
God's covenant. He is faithful to it, about His promise. God
always does what He ought to do, namely, fulfill His promise.
That is why His righteousness can be expressed in judgment,
or in salvation."

But as for me, I will hope continually,

And will praise Thee yet more and more.

My mouth shall tell of Thy righteousness,

And of Thy salvation all day long.

For I do not know the sum of them.

I will come with the mighty deeds of the Lord God; I will
make mention of Thy righteousness, Thine alone.

Psalm 71: 14-16.

The psalmists proclaim God's justice in Psalms 9, 71,103,
and 111.

Psalms 9:1 "I will praise You, O Lord, with my whole heart;
I will show forth (recount and tell aloud) all Your marvelous

works and wonderful deeds! 2 I will rejoice in You and be in high spirits; I will sing praise to Your name, O Most High! 3 When my enemies turned back, they stumbled and perished before You. 4 For You have maintained my right and my cause; You sat on the throne judging righteously."

5 "You have rebuked the nations; you have destroyed the wicked; You have blotted out their name forever and ever.

Psalms 71:5 For You are my hope; O Lord God, you are my trust from my youth and the source of my confidence.

Psalms 103:8,9, 8 The Lord is merciful and gracious, slow to anger and plenteous in mercy and loving-kindness.

9 He will not always chide or be contending, neither will He keep His anger forever or hold a grudge.

Psalms 111:7 The works of His hands are [absolute] truth and justice [faithful and right]; and all His decrees and precepts are sure (fixed, established, and trustworthy)."

Note these words from another famous author.

He will declare or pronounce judgment; He will execute the office of judge. To all people, to the nations of the earth… and the declaration is that in His dealings with dwellers on the earth He will be guided by the strictest principles of justice….

He will not be influenced by partiality; He will show no favoritism; He will not be bribed. He will do exact justice to all. Albert Barnes;

God is a refuge to the poor, to the widows, to the orphans, and a refuge for you and me. We have that assurance that when, in times of trouble, when everything in our lives is in turmoil and we don't know which way to turn, we can say

He is my fortress and refuge and confidant; one I can put my trust in. We have only to call out His name and have the assurance that our Heavenly Father will answer our call and meet our every need.

2 Samuel 22:3 My God, my Rock, in Him will I take refuge; my Shield and the Horn of my salvation; my Stronghold and my Refuge, my Savior—You save me from violence.

Psalms 18:2 "The Lord is my Rock, my Fortress, and my Deliverer; my God, my keen and firm Strength in Whom I will trust and take refuge, my Shield, and the Horn of my salvation, my High Tower.

Psalms 27:1 The Lord is my Light and my Salvation— whom shall I fear or dread? The Lord is the Refuge and Stronghold of my life—of whom shall I be afraid?"

We should have no reason to fear or be wondering how we are going to get through any situation when we have the realization that Father God is our refuge and know He has our back in every situation of life all we have to do is call out His name, and the problem is taken care of. Amen!

God is Faithful! If you wish to see how faithful God is try Him; simply call out His name in any situation and you will find He is there waiting to help you through any problem.

Deuteronomy 7:9 "Know, recognize and understand therefore that the Lord your God, He is God, the faithful God, who keeps covenant and steadfast love and mercy with those who love Him and keep His commandments, to a thousand generations."

Deuteronomy 32:4 "He is the Rock, His work is perfect, for all His ways are law and justice. A God of faithfulness without breach or deviation of just and right is He."

1 Corinthians 1:9 God is faithful (reliable, trustworthy, and therefore ever true to His promise, and He can be depended on); by Him, you were called into companionship and participation with His Son, Jesus Christ our Lord.

Remember Satan is a liar and the father of lies. The Word says he comes to kill, steal and destroy. But Father God is there always to build you up and to set your feet on the solid rock which is Christ Jesus. So many times, we as people of faith, lose sight of what the Word tells us. We ask for help with finances, healing, and problems with our children or other loved ones. But when God does not answer our request immediately we get all bent out of shape and start thinking He isn't going to answer our prayer. We start to doubt and our faith wavers, often we go so far as to say I don't have faith in that. We should never speak this into our lives, you should say I am the righteousness of God. I can do all things through Christ Jesus who strengthens me. I am above and not beneath; I am the head and not the tail. Christ is my high tower on whom I can trust and rely. We are heirs and joint heirs with Jesus to the throne. If we can remember this and every time our faith starts to waver speak these words into our lives our faith will be renewed in Christ Jesus. AMEN.

Matthew 11:28 "Come to Me, all you who labor and are heavy-laden and overburdened, and I will cause you to rest." [I will ease and relieve and refresh your souls.]

Regardless of what happens, we need to do what the song-writer penned so many years ago and know and believe that what our Lord tells us is true. Just hold on.

The song says,

Turn your eyes upon Jesus

Look straight into His wonderful face

And the things of this world will grow strangely dime

In the light of His glory and grace. Amen

We survive because of faith not because we have extraordinary stamina but because God is righteous. Christian discipleship is a process of paying more and more attention to God's righteousness and less and less attention to our own; finding the meaning of our lives not by probing our moods and motives and morals but by believing God's will and purpose; making a map of the faithfulness of God, not charting the rise and fall of our enthusiasms. It is out of such a reality that we acquire perseverance.

By: Eugene Peterson

In closing remember,

God is Righteous

God is Trustworthy

God is our Refuge

God is Faithful

AMEN

Rev. Bruce Pero

CHAPTER 18
End Times Revelation Eight

1 Thessalonians 4:16-18 Amplified Bible,16 "For the Lord Himself will come down from heaven with a shout of command, with the voice of the archangel and with the [blast of the] trumpet of God, and the dead in Christ will rise first. 17 Then we who are alive and remain [on the earth] will simultaneously be caught up (raptured) (the bible says, caught away) together with them [the resurrected ones] in the clouds to meet the Lord in the air, and so we will always be with the Lord!"

18 "Therefore comfort and encourage one another with these words [concerning our reunion with believers who have died].

Luke 21:25-36 Amplified Bible, 25 And there will be signs in the sun and moon and stars; and upon the earth [there will be] distress (trouble and anguish) of nations in bewilderment and perplexity [without resources, left wanting, embarrassed, in doubt, not knowing which way to turn] at the roaring (the echo) of the tossing of the sea. 26 Men swooning away with dread and apprehension and expectation of the things that are coming on the world; for the [very] powers of the heavens will be shaken and caused to totter. Matthew 24:8 But all these things are merely the be inning of birth pangs [of the earth in its intolerable anguish and the time of unprecedented trouble]". We are seeing these things taking place as we speak and watch what is taking place in our world in 2022, from the Euphrates River drying up at the end of 2021, referenced in Revelations 16:12, "And the sixth angel poured out his vial upon the great river Euphrates; and the water thereof was dried up, that the way of the kings of the east might be prepared."

Luke 21:27-36 (Amplified Classic version) "And then they will see the Son of Man coming in a cloud with great (transcendent and overwhelming) power and [all His kingly] glory (majesty and splendor). 28 Now when these things begin to occur, look up and lift up your heads because your redemption (deliverance) is drawing near. 29 And He told them a parable: Look at the fig tree and all the trees; 30 When they put forth their buds and come out in leaf, you see for yourselves and perceive and know that summer is a ready near."

31 "Even so, when you see these things taking place, understand and know that the kingdom of God is at hand. 32 Assuredly I tell you, this generation (those living at that definite period) will not perish and pass away until all has taken place. 33 The sky and earth (the universe, the world) will pass away, but My words will not pass away. 34 But take heed to yourselves and be on your guard, lest your hearts be

overburdened and depressed (weighed down) with the gid-diness and headache and nausea of self-indulgence, drunk-enness, and worldly worries and cares about [the business of] this life, and [lest] that day come upon you suddenly like a trap or a noose; 35 For it will come up all who live upon the face of the entire earth." 36 "Keep awake then and watch at all times [be discreet, attentive, and ready], praying that you may have the full strength and ability and be accounted worthy to escape all these things [taken together] that will take place, and to stand in the presence of the Son of Man." The lamb Breaks the Seventh Seal.

Revelation 8 Amplified Bible the Seventh Seal—the Trumpets 8 "When He (the Lamb) broke open the seventh seal, there was silence in heaven for about half an hour [in awe of God's impending judgment]. 2 Then I saw the seven angels who stand before God, and seven trumpets were given to them. 3 Another angel came and stood at the altar.

He had a golden censer, and much incense was given to him so that he might add it to the prayers of all the saints (God's people) on the golden altar in front of the throne."

4 "And the smoke and fragrant aroma of the incense, with the prayers of the saints (God's people), ascended before God from the angel's hand. 5 So the angel took the censer and filled it with fire from the altar, and hurled it to the earth, and there were peals of thunder and loud rumblings and sounds and flashes of lightning and an earthquake. 6 Then the seven angels with the seven trumpets prepared to sound them [initiating the judgments]."

7 "The first [angel] sounded [his trumpet], and there was [a storm of] hail and fire, mixed with blood, and it was hurled to the earth; and a third of the earth was burned up, and a third of the trees were burned up, and all the green grass was burned up.

8 The second angel sounded [his trumpet], and something like a great mountain blazing with fire was hurled into the sea, and a third of the sea was turned to blood;

9 And a third of the living creatures that were in the sea died, and a third of the ships were destroyed." 10 "The third angel sounded [his trumpet], and a great star fell from heaven, burning like a torch [flashing across the sky], and it fell on a third of the rivers and on the springs of [fresh] waters. 11 The name of the star is Wormwood, and a third of the water became wormwood, and many people died from the waters because they had become bitter (toxic).

12 Then the fourth angel sounded [his trumpet], and a third of the sun and a third of the moon and a third of the stars were struck, so that a third of them would be darkened and a third of the daylight would not shine, and the night in the same way [would not shine].

13 Then I looked, and I heard a solitary eagle flying in mid-heaven [for all to see], saying with a loud voice, "Woe, woe, woe [great wrath is coming] to those who dwell on the earth,

because of the remaining blasts of the trumpets which the three angels are about to sound [announcing ever greater judgments]!"

Tom Horn was called by God to be a Prophetic voice to the world, in the very days, we are living in. At the age of 21, Tom Horn was given a vision, He went to heaven. God gave him a vision, but he was to forget the message until a later date. Later when Ton Horn retired God revealed to him 12 points of the vision, he had at 21. The vision Tom had in 2010 was that Pope Benedict was to resign on April 13, 2012. This is something that has never happened before in history. When Tom told his prophecy, people suggested that he should not tell such a thing as it would ruin his credibility. This had never happened in the history of the Vatican. But there was a news release from the Vatican in March of 2012. that the Pope had put in his resignation, and it was excepted on April 13th, 2012. Tom Horn's second prophecy is concerning an Asteroid that is to hit the earth in 2029. Upon hearing this Donald Trump set up a task force to monitor the Asteroids that are coming near the earth. But there is one that will be seen by a telescope in 2024 and you will be able to see it with your naked eye in 2025. The name of the Asteroid is called Apophis. It was named after an Egyptian God called Apophis. This Asteroid is to come into our atmosphere and strike the earth on April 13th, 2029. Remember (Revelation 8:10, the Asteroid is the size of four football fields and is traveling at 28,000 miles per hour. One-half will go into the sea, killing one-third of the plant life, also one-third of the fish, and will destroy any ships in that area. The second half of the Asteroid will hit between New Mexico and California.

10's of thousands will be killed. The impact will be equivalent to 65 thousand atomic bombs detonated in the same spot; quite possibly cracking the earth's mantle.

Tom Horn talked about the Asteroid hitting the fault line in California where there has been volcanic activity in the past; the ground erupts spewing ash and smoke into the atmosphere and blocking out the sun, moon, and part of the stars.

If we take all these events into consideration with the time of the tribulation it is quite possible we could be coming into that very period. The asteroid will hit the earth in April 2029, backing it up 7 years, accounting for the tribulation period, we're looking at 2022 or thereabout.

Chapter 18 is credited to Tom Horn.

Rev. Bruce Pero
06/14/2021

♡

CHAPTER 19
Light Of the Spirit

I believe it was in late September 2009, when I was asked to sit on the search committee to find a new pastor for our church. The board for the church had called me to let me know that there would be a meeting with the superintendent of our district on the last Saturday of the month. I am a firm believer in prayer, so when I got the call for our meeting I immediately started praying, asking the Lord to guide us in our search for a new pastor. With help from the Superintendent, a list of candidates was in process. As I have always done, I went into my office to start the day off, I would read scriptures, pray, and listen to praise and worship music. Suddenly, right in front of me, there was a vision so real.

I was standing at the doors to the sanctuary when all of a sudden

a bright, white light descended down through the roof of the church right in the middle of the seats. I could not believe it. I was standing at the entrance to the sanctuary of our church in Verona, Ontario when it hit and exploded.

Wave after wave rolled out from the center of the light. The light was so bright you could not look directly at it. Then as I watched, I could actually see the waves going out through the walls of the church and across the lawns and streets as far as I could see. The light was the outpouring of the Holy Spirit on the church. On the waves were God's People taking the message of God's saving grace into the surrounding communities.

Also, the light striking the church was to show that God wants to use His church; I believe God wants a new thing to be birthed in His church, a new way of worship. I believe God is calling His church back to true worship, in spirit and in truth.

God is getting ready to bring the remnant together that He spoke of; to build his church for eternity.

The question is, are you going to be part of His church, the bride of Christ, without a spot or wrinkle? You can be; just ask Him into your heart, accepting Him as your Lord and Savior. Jesus said, "ALL that call on my name will be saved." AMEN. Remember this vision was in September 2009, it was recorded on January 2ND 2010. Now let's jump ahead to the outbreak of the Covid pandemic in November 2020. Most churches closed under the direction of the local health departments, and that decision is still being talked about. But the little church in Verona stood its ground, following the guidelines handed down, holding church as much as they could.

In the summer of 2021, actually starting about June this little church moved its services out into its parking lot and held the drive-in church.

Not only that, but they built a brand-new gazebo, complete with a roof, and the platform was big enough for their piano player and guitar players plus praise and worship singers. It was amazing. By July the parking lot was full of churchgoers, and their amen was done with the honking of their horns. Some requests were coming from neighbors across the street and next door to turn up the sound so they could enjoy the service from their decks and patios.

So, you see the vision I had in September 2009 has finally come to fruition. The gospel is being taken into the community, in the small town of Verona Ontario. So, I believe what the devil meant for evil God over-ruled for good; to further get the Gospel out into the world. Amen!

Revised on August 17, 2021.
By: Rev Bruce Pero

CHAPTER 20
The Gate Keepers

As a child growing up on a farm, these words meant so many different things. The gatekeeper on the farm was the person that was given the task of manning the gate going into the pasture where we would put our cows to grass for the day or night between milking. Today, I want to share with you about another type of gatekeeper. This type of gate-keeping job could affect the rest of your life or the outcome at the least. This type of gate keeping is the keeping or guarding of our hearts to accomplish the holiness, the very righteousness that God has promised us and called us to be.

Luke 1:74 "To grant us that we, being rescued from the hand of our enemies, might serve Him without fear,"

75 "In holiness [being set apart] and righteousness [being upright] before Him all our days."

Matthew 6:33 "But first and most importantly seek (aim at, strive after) His kingdom and His righteousness [His way of doing and being right—the attitude and character of God], and all these things will be given to you also."

Luke 6:45 "A good man out of the good treasure of his heart bringeth forth that which is good, and an evil man out of the evil treasure of his heart bringeth forth that which is evil: for of the abundance of the heart, his mouth speaks." We are not just gatekeepers, but God has called us to be a watchman on the wall, to be ever vigilant, and to sound the alarm when the enemy is approaching.

Isaiah 62:6-7 "I have set watchmen upon thy walls, O Jerusalem, which shall never hold their Peace Day nor night: ye that make mention of the Lord, keep not silence, and give him no rest, till he establishes, and till he makes Jerusalem a praise in the earth."

God is looking for a people to be gatekeepers, that will be ever vigilant and display a life of holiness and also display the very righteousness of God.

1 John 3:3 "And everyone who has this hope [confidently placed] in Him purifies himself, just as He is pure (holy, undefiled, guiltless)."

Psalms 24:3-5 "Who shall go up into the mountain of the Lord! Or who shall stand in His Holy Place!

Who may stand in His Holy Temple!

Or who may stand in His Presence!"

4: "He who has clean hands and a pure heart, who has not lifted himself up to falsehood or to what is false, nor sworn deceitfully."

When we pursue the answer to these specific questions, we need only to reflect back on what God's word says. When you have done all there is to stand then stand and occupy until I come." (Occupy in Greek is a military term.)

Psalms 139:14 "I will give thanks and praise to You, for I am fearfully and wonderfully made; Wonderful are Your works, and my soul knows it very well."

Breaking down Psalms 24:3-5 to clarify its meanings.

Clean hands: translations are, empty, translucent, salted, and flawless.

Who has not worshiped idols?

The Idols in our lives can be represented by a multitude of things, cars, houses, money, and people in different positions either of authority or in the entertainment world.

Who has not made promises in the name of a false god? Who has not made something to be more important than their walk with God.

The meaning of a Pure Heart: Beloved, empty, freedom, clear, to be innocent, clean flawless.

Falschood/Vanity: Bearer of untrue testimony, sinful treachery. (Vanity): trouble, wickedness, emptiness, worthlessness.

Deceitfully: To act covertly, to deride, mock, fraud, treachery.

Have we really taken inventory of our lives looking at these things that were just mentioned? It is time we started to take the word of God at face value. It is time to start living the Word of God not just reading it and or leaving it sitting on the coffee table collecting dust.

We hear people say, oh I know what's in the Bible. I don't need to read it every day. The Bible tells us very clearly, in Romans 10:17 "So then faith comes by hearing, and hearing by the word of God." (Also, when you read God's word read it out loud so that your faith will be built up by you hearing the word of God.

God's word tells us.... "It is a lamp unto our feet.

Psalms 119:105 Your word is a lamp to my feet and a light to my path." God's word is our manual for our lives, our directional compass.

So, we are gatekeepers and watchmen on the wall guarding God's word, being doers of His word, not just listeners. We will receive what God's word tells us in Psalms 24:5.

5: "He shall receive blessing from the Lord and righteousness from the God of his salvation."

Look in the next scripture. It is telling us we are the generation that will pursue Him and seek His face.

6 This is the generation [description] of those who seek Him [who inquire of and for Him and of necessity require Him], who seek Your face, [O God of] Jacob. Selah [pause and think of that]!

As we draw near to the end, the Lord is encouraging His people to look up, and press in, the king is coming, He says.

7 "Lift up you, heads, O you gates; and be lifted up, you age-abiding doors, that the King of glory may come in. 8 Who is the King of glory? The Lord is strong and mighty, the Lord is mighty in battle. 9 Lift up your heads, O you, gates; yes, lift them up, you age-abiding doors, that the King of glory may come in.10 Who is [He then] this King of glory? The Lord of hosts, He is the King of glory."

So, in closing, always remember that we are the gatekeepers, the watchman on the wall, ensuring that the word of God gets out there, to a lost and dying world. Matthew

9;37 Then He (Jesus) said to His disciples, "The harvest is [indeed] plentiful, but the workers are few. 38 So pray to the Lord of the harvest to send out workers into His harvest."

These workers in today's world are you and me. So, I ask you where will you spend eternity? There are really only two choices, heaven or hell. My prayer for you today is that you choose Heaven. Jesus said, "All that call upon my name will be saved." Acts 2:21 "And it shall come to pass, that whosoever shall call on the name of the Lord shall be saved."

In closing, if you would like to know today that you will be spending eternity in heaven repeat this prayer. "Jesus, I ask you into my heart, I ask you to forgive me of all my sin. I believe you died on the cross for me and on the third day, you arose from the dead. I make you Lord of my Life."

If you prayed this prayer, you are born again and on your way to heaven, I will look for you there. Amen!!

Rev Bruce Pero
February 10/2022

♡

CHAPTER 21
The Reality of Redemption

What is the difference between theological redemption and Christ's actual redemptive work!

In answering this question, I would like to look at two words, the first is redemption, the second is redeemed, our source is the Webster dictionary. The first is (redemption), Redemption has been a theological word in the minds of most believers. It means in English, distinction, deliverance, ransom payment, and ransom in full.

The second word is (redeemed), which means to be next of kin, ransom; to release, to break off or crunch; to deliver. You remember that the keyword for Romans is righteousness, or the ability to stand in the father's presence without a sense of guilt or inferiority; stand there without condemnation or the sense of sin consciousness.

That could not be as long as we were under the dominion of the enemy. It could not be as long as that enemy's nature was in our spirit; so there must come Redemption from the nature of Satan and redemption from the fear of Satan and of his work.

So, the Spirit through the Apostle, tells us a Righteousness has been discovered; has come to light, and that Righteousness comes to man through faith in Jesus Christ, and belongs to all those who acknowledge Christ as Savior and confess Him as their Lord. They are Justified, REDEEMED on the grounds of GRACE, through the Redemption that God worked in, or through Christ.

That Redemption or payment is based upon the fact that God laid our sins and diseases upon Jesus that, "Him who knew no sin.

God made Christ become sin so that we might become the Righteousness of God in Him." How does Christ's sitting at the Right Hand of the Father affect us?

Romans 6:14, "For sin shall not (any longer) exert dominion over you, since now you are not under the law (as slaves), but under grace (as subjects of God's favor and mercy)."

Colossians 1:13, 14, (The Father)... "has delivered and drawn us to Himself out of the control and dominion of darkness and has transferred us into the Kingdom of the Son of His love."

14, "Jesus, in whom we have our redemption through His blood, (which means) the forgiveness of our sins."

Hebrews 9:11, 12, "But (that appointed time came) when Christ (the Messiah) appeared as a High Priest of the better things that have come and are to come. (Then) through the greater and more perfect tabernacle not made with (human) hands, that is, not a part of this material creation. 12, "He went once for all into the (Holy of) Hollies (of heaven), not by the blood of goats and calves (by which to make reconciliation between God and man), but his own blood, having found and secured a complete redemption (an everlasting release for us." Christ not only obtained Eternal Redemption for us, but He sat down at the Right Hand of the Majesty on high. He carried His blood into the Holy of Hollies, and our Redemption was sealed.

What does Jesus' victory over Satan mean to us?

The Supreme Court of the Universe passed upon it and declared that whosoever accepted Jesus as Savior and confessed Him as Lord could come into God's family and be free from condemnation. Satan is eternally defeated. That Redemption is an Eternal Redemption. God wrought it in His Son. That His Son satisfied the claim of justice. That Son is sealed at the head of the New Creation at the Right Hand of the Father, and the New Creation is free from the dominion of Satan. Christ is the head. You will enjoy your rights in this Redemption as you know its reality.

Explain Hebrews 9:15, "(Christ the Messiah) is, therefore, the negotiator and the mediator of an (entirely) new agreement (testament, covenant), so that those who are called and offered it may receive the fulfillment of the promised everlasting inheritance." His death rescues and delivers and redeems them from the transgressions committed under the (old) first agreement."

We should realize that Christ is our negotiator and mediator; He sits on the right side of the Father interceding for us.

It is also important that we know that Christ's death on the Cross and His substitution or sacrifice not only met our needs, but it reached back and canceled all the promissory notes of that first covenant so that every man that believed in the blood of bulls and goats and was covered by that blood was perfectly redeemed by the blood of Jesus that He carried into the Holy of hollies.

They were redeemed as servants; we are redeemed as sons.

Hebrews 9:26, "For then would He often have to suffer (over and over again) since the foundation of the world. But as it now is, He has once and for all at the consummation and close of the age appeared to put away and abolish sin by His sacrifice of Himself."

As long as one holds his redemption as a theory or as a doctrine it will bring him no sense of reality, but as soon as we look up and say, "Father, I thank Thee for my perfect Redemption, that this body of mine and senses are no longer to be dominated by the adversary. I'm free, and by Your grace, I will not be entangled again in the yoke of bondage." When we realize this then, it is real.

Explain the expression, "Jesus is the Firstborn from among the dead."

Colossians 1:18, He is also the head of (His) body, the church;" seeing He is the beginning, the firstborn from among the dead

so that He alone in everything and in every respect might occupy the chief place (stand first and be per-eminent).

Jesus was made sin with our sin. He became our substitute. We died with Him. We were buried with Him. We were judged by Him. He went to the place where we should have gone, and He suffered there until the claims of justice against us were met; until all the claims were satisfied. Then the grave could not hold Him any longer.

1st Peter 3:18, "For Christ (the Messiah Himself), died for sin once and for all, the righteous for the unrighteous (the Just for the unjust, the Innocent for the guilty), that He might bring us to God." In His human body, He was put to death, but He was made alive in the spirit.

Then, before He arose from the dead, He conquered Satan as our substitute. After Satan was conquered, and his authority broken, Jesus arose from the dead.

You see, the difference between the natural birth and the New Birth is that one of them physical, and the other, is spiritual. 2nd Corinthians 5:17, "Therefore if any person is (en-grafted) in Christ (the Messiah) he is a new creation (a new creature altogether); the old (previous moral and spiritual condition) has passed away. Behold the fresh and new comes."

Also, read Romans 6:1-16

Where does the Word tell us that sin had been put away?

Christ gave Paul the Revelation of His grace. This revelation is an unveiling of the finished work of Christ that is consummated in the new birth.

You understand that all the plans of God were unveiled to us in the First Covenant. He is pointing to the great event when God on legal grounds can impart to man His Own Nature and make him a new creation. You can see how the forgiveness of sins would not touch the issue, that the confirming of a child by a priest could not reach the issue.

There must be a New Creation through the forgiveness of sin.

That child must receive Eternal Life; the Nature of God, for the natural man is without God. He is without hope, and he is in the world. He is Satan-ruled.

We must understand the difference between forgiveness and the remission of sins. A man receives forgiveness of sins after he is Born Again, as often as he sins, this does not give us a license to continually sin because all we have to do is ask for His forgiveness. Jesus said to the woman caught in adultery when everyone had left, "Where are your accusers?" She replied, "They are all gone." Jesus said, "Neither do I condemn you, go and sin no more." You remember 1st John 1:9, "If we confess our sins, He is faithful and righteous to forgive us our sins, and to cleanse us from all unrighteousness."

In doing this, God is putting our sins away, into the sea of forgetfulness, NEVER to be remembered again. This means your name is written in the Lamb's Book of Life and you are on your way to heaven. Amen.

Rev Bruce Pero

CHAPTER 22
The Word Coming Alive in Us

What does God's Living Word do in us?

It gives us assurance of eternal life. It brings us to the right standing with God. The living Word in us builds our Faith. It gives us Hope for Tomorrow: The living Word in us develops our Christian character and our walk with the Lord. Without the Living Word in us, we would fail in our walk with Jesus.

What Romans 10:11 means to us in our daily Life.

The scripture says, "No man that believes in Him (who adheres to, relies on, and trusts in Him) will be put to shame or be disappointed." In today's world, it means the same as it did back then, regardless of who we are Jew or Gentile. We are His children; we will never be put to shame for believing in Jesus but shall receive what He has promised.

Verse,13, Promises that everyone who calls upon the name of the Lord (invoking Him as Lord) (will) be saved. We are in His Kingdom. Colossians 1:13, "The Father" has delivered and drawn us to Himself out of the control and the dominion of darkness and has transferred us into the Kingdom of the Son of His love." We have found His Righteousness. 2nd Corinthians 5:21, "For He hath made Him be sin for us, who knew no sin; that we might be made the Righteousness of God in Him."

God's promise to us, His children, is made very clear in Romans 8: 14-16, "For all who are led by the spirit of God, are Sons of God. 15, For (the spirit which) you have now received (is) not a spirit of slavery to put you once more in bondage to fear, but you have received the spirit of adoption (the Spirit producing sonship) in (the bliss of) which we cry, Abba (Father)!"

16, "The spirit Himself (thus) testifies together with our own spirit, (assuring us) that we are children of God." And in 1st John 3:1 we read, "Behold what manner of love the Father has bestowed upon us, that we should be called the sons of God, therefore the world knows us not, because it knew Him not. And not only are we sons and daughters, but we are heirs of God and joint heirs with Jesus Christ." God is our actual Father.

John 16:27, "For the Father Himself (tenderly) loves you because you have loved Me and have believed that I came out from the Father."

If we are His children and if He is our Father, then He is responsible for us. If we take our place as Sons and daughters, He is bound to take His place as our Father.

What is our responsibility to Him as our Heavenly Father?

Our responsibility is to walk in His love, to show His love to everyone we meet, be doers of the Word, not just hearers, and to lift our heavenly Father up in praise and worship in

EVERYTHING we do. John 14: 23, Jesus answered, "If a person (really) loves Me he will keep My Word (obey My teachings): and My Father will love him, and We will come to him and make Our home (abode, special dwelling place) with him. If a man loves Me, he will keep My Word." That means we are taking our place as sons and daughters. Also, we will take responsibility as sons and daughters, and we will enjoy the privileges of it. If we do that, then He will assume His place as a Father and will make His home with us, take care of us and enable us to meet our obligations, enable us to walk in love and in wisdom and to walk in the fullness of His fellowship.

What are the benefits of this righteousness? The benefits are that we have the knowledge that we are His sons and daughters and that He loved us so much that He sent His Son to die for us.

That He has adopted us into His family and made us heirs and joint heirs to His Kingdom.

2 Timothy 4:8 "Henceforth there is laid up for me a crown of righteousness, which the Lord, the righteous Judge, shall give me at that day: and not to me only, but unto all of them also that love His appearing."

In Philippians 4:13, "I have strength for all things in Christ who empowers me. I am ready for anything and equal to anything, through Him who infuses inner strength into me." I am self-sufficient in Christ's sufficiency. Here is the ability of God that becomes ours the moment that we come into the Family. Philippians 4:19 reads, "And my God will liberally supply (fill to the full) your every need according to

His riches in glory in Christ Jesus." (That will be the end of worry, the end of fear. That will mean that God, our Father, has assumed the responsibility that came to Him when He gave us Eternal Life.

Proverbs 3:5,6, "Lean on, trust in, and be confident in the Lord with all your heart and mind and do not rely on your own insight or understanding. 6, In all your ways know, recognize and acknowledge Him, and He will direct and make straight and plain your paths."

What are His children equipped with?

We as His children are equipped with the Living Word of God, with the knowledge that we walk in His love and wisdom. He has made us be His righteousness, He is saying to us, I want your heart trust, your fullest confidence. I want you to learn that I am your wisdom and your ability. I can make you wiser than your enemies. I can make you master over circumstances.

Philippians 4:11, "Not that I speak in respect of want for I have learned, in whatsoever state I am, therewith to be content."

He wants us to know that we have His ability to deal will all circumstances.

2nd Corinthians 3:4,5, Such is the reliance and confidence that we have through Christ toward and concerning God.

5, Not that we are fit (qualified and sufficient in ability) of ourselves to form personal judgments or to claim or count anything as coming from us, but our power and ability and sufficiency are from God.

What is the vocation or life's purpose of God's children?

Let us first take a look at the meaning of the word (vocation)

In Strong's Dictionary, it tells us Vocation's meaning is invitation or station in Life. So, in your vocation as one of God's children, you have His ability in Life, to fight the good fight of Faith, and take the invitation of the Good News to the office, in the store, to the schoolroom, in the home, and to the streets. The mechanic has His wisdom at the bench. The Judge and the Lawyer both have access to His ability. There isn't a station in life in which the believer finds himself, but God's ability is not with him, (or her) and his Father is not watching over him, meeting his every need in every situation.

Psalms 27:1, "The Lord is my Light and my salvation whom shall I fear or dread? The Lord is the Refuge and Stronghold of my Life of whom shall I be afraid?" The promise is ours in keeping Malachi 3:10, "Bring ye all the tithes into the storehouse, that there may be meat in mine house, and prove me now herewith, saith the Lord of hosts, if I will not open you the windows of heaven, and pour you out a blessing, that there shall not be room enough to receive it."

(Our Fearless Song) Psalms 46:1, "God is our Refuge and Strength (mighty and impenetrable to temptation), a very present and well-proved help in trouble." (He can meet every financial obligation when you trust Him with all your heart.

But it will be necessary for you to go into business with Jesus, to trust Him, for you to be partners.

Malachi 3:10,11, "Bring all the tithes (the whole tenth of your income) into the storehouse, that there may be food in My house, and PROVE Me now by it, says the Lord of Hosts if I will not open the windows of Heaven for you and pour you out a blessing, that there shall not be room enough to receive it."

Now you people that have not been able to meet your obligations: you have had to make, and get loans, had sickness and expenses that should not have come to you. Notice verse 11, it is for you. "And I will rebuke the devourer for your sake, and he shall not destroy the fruits of your ground; neither shall your vines cast her fruit before the time in the field."

Satan has tried to keep you in bondage with one thing after another that has happened, that has kept your pocketbook drained. Now the Father has promised to watch over your finances so that you will have no unnecessary bills to meet. If you have fearless confidence in Him, He will see that blessings shower upon you. But if you waver, trust Him today and doubt Him tomorrow, you will find yourself walking alone in your circumstances. God wants us to have unwavering faith, love, and trust in His ability to see us through all situations in life.

We see in God's word, from the covenant that was written in Isaiah 41:10 when God is speaking to Jacob and then in 1st John 4:4.

When you know that you are connected to Him and that He has your back, it gives you a sense of security. Isaiah 41:10, We find the Lord speaking to Jacob, "Fear thou not; for I am with thee: be not dismayed; for I am thy God: I will strengthen thee; I will help thee, I will uphold thee with the right hand of my righteousness."

Notice this sentence. "I am with thee." He is in your home with you. He is in the shop with you; He is in the school with you.

"Fear thou not for I am God almighty, Creator of the universe.

I am your father; you are my child, and I am watching over you. Be not dismayed, for I am your God."

That statement thrills my soul, "I am thy God, thy Father, the strength of your Life, your wisdom, your ability."

And then He whispers, "I will strengthen you, no matter what your work may be. If it is physical strength, He is your sufficiency. If it is mental strength, He meets you.

And if it is the spiritual strength that will give you the courage to face impossibilities, He is there. You notice, "I am with you," but that is in the Old Covenant. Now He says, In 1st John 4:4, "Little children, you are of God (you belong to Him) and have (already) defeated and overcome them (the agents of the anti-Christ), because He Who lives in you is greater (mightier) than he who is in the world" God loves you so much as one of His children, His only desire is that you spend eternity with Him in Heaven one day. So why not ask Him into your heart today to be Lord of your life, knowing you will spend eternity with Him? It is so simple, Jesus said, "All that call on my name will be saved." Believe me, your life will never be the same. If you do this, remember to read your Bible every day and don't forget to take time to talk to your Heavenly Father. He will be expecting to hear from you. Amen!!!

Blessings
Rev. Bruce Pero

CHAPTER 23
Judged And Condemned

As I look back through the pages of my life, I see all the times someone has made condemning accusations. Things I may or may not have done. These are accusations that could have changed the outcome of my life. Have you ever had people accuse you of things you know you did not do? It can be very humiliating, not to mention embarrassing. Look what God's word has to say about passing judgments, which I might add, is no different than condemning or making accusations about others, very hurtful things. These things could do irreversible damage for the rest of one's life.

Matthew 7Judging Others "Do not judge and criticize and condemn [others unfairly with an attitude of self-righteous superiority as though assuming the office of a judge], so that you will not be judged [unfairly]. For just as you [hypocritically] judge others [when you are sinful and unrepentant], so will you be judged; and by your standard of measure [used to pass out judgment], judgment will be measured to you. Why do you look at the [insignificant] speck in your brother's eye, but not notice and acknowledge the log in your own eye?"

I would like to use a quote from Rev. Robert DeGrandis, S.S.J. We'll title it Meditation. Picture Jesus standing before you. Jesus is wearing the bloodstained robe put upon Him by the mocking soldiers after the scourging. See the crown of thorns plaited tightly upon His head cutting deeply into His scalp, matting his hair with blood. Look into the eyes of Jesus. See the compassionate, deep, brown eyes of Jesus glazed with pain, yet filled with love. Walk over to where Jesus is standing and allow Him to place His arms around you.

Also picture before you the person out of your past that has condemned you, labeled you, misjudged you, and deeply hurt you. As that person now stands before you, Jesus takes your hand placing it into the hand of the condemning person. Jesus says, "For My sake forgive this person. Forgive even as I have forgiven." This is one of the most compassionate and heartfelt pictures I have ever got to view in my mind. In closing look at another scripture that God's word has for us concerning Judging. Then I want to ask you to meditate on what you have read and see if it doesn't change your life. John 3:18 "Whoever believes and has decided to trust in Him [as personal Savior and Lord] is not judged [for this one, there is no judgment, no rejection, no condemnation]; but the one who does not believe [and has decided to reject Him as personal Savior and Lord] is judged already [that one has been convicted and sentenced], because he has not believed and trusted in the name of the [One and] only begotten Son of God [the One who is truly unique, the only

One of His kind, the One who alone can save him]". Jesus said a new commandment I give you, see it in the scripture. John 13:34 "I am giving you a new commandment, that you love one another just as I have loved you," So you too are to love one another. 35 "By this everyone will know that you are My disciples if you have love and unselfish concern for one another." My prayer for you is that it will make a difference in your life as it has in mine. Amen!!!!

Rev. Bruce Pero

CHAPTER 24
A New Commandment I Give You

Many scholars have debated down through the ages concerning the commandments, saying the only commandments given, officially were the Ten Commandments. These are still kept and are a vital part of our lives and always should be. Then our Lord and Savior were born and with that birth, He brought some additions to the commandments we are to live by. For example, Paul wrote a new one in Romans 12;2 "Don't copy the behavior and customs of this world, but let God transform you into a new person by changing the way you think. Then you will learn to know God's will for you, which is good and pleasing and perfect."

This is telling us not to live as the world lives, but we are to pattern ourselves after Jesus' life, renewing our minds by studying God's word, so we can be in the perfect will of God. Then Jesus gave us another commandment that would change our lives forever.

It is found in, John 13:34 "A new commandment I give unto you, that ye love one another; as I have loved you, that ye also love one another."

Knowing the Master is not just knowing stories from the Bible but having a personal relationship with the Him. Can you say you have a personal relationship with the Master? Do you talk with Him daily? Can you say, you know that still small voice that calls out to you in the early morning or late at night; the voice that says, "It will be OK, I have you in the palm of my hand." When you are going through problems, knowing His Shekinah Glory can only be experienced by having a deep-rooted relationship with our Lord and Savior Jesus Christ. Amen!

One of the most astounding scriptures, to help us know the Master and His love for everyone in the world, is found in John 3:16 (K J V), "For God so loved and dearly prized the world, that He gave His only begotten Son so that whoever believes and trusts in Him shall not perish but have eternal life." In the last two years, I have been so blessed, serving as Chaplain for South Frontenac Community Services. Seeing the expressions on people's faces, as I get to share the gospel of the saving knowledge of Jesus Christ with them is such a blessing. But not only that, my Heavenly Father has shown His love to me in so many ways and has drawn me to such an amazing closeness with Him.

He has brought me through some serious health issues and is continuing to work in my life. This spiritual closeness I am talking about only comes by getting to know the Master on a personal level. This relationship is offered to all and anyone willing to press in, as close as possible, to our Lord. To literally hold onto the Masters's hand and say, "I will not let go until you bless me," is knowing all about my Lord. I encourage you to try it. Take hold of the Masters's hand, draw close to Him and He will draw close to you because He loves us all with a never-ending love. Amen!Romans 6:5(K J V), "For if we have been planted together in the likeness of his death, we shall be also in the likeness of his resurrection:" As Christ died for us, He became one with us. He died for all mankind. He took everyone's place on the cross. That means when He died, we died. We became one with Him on the cross and in His death. He did all this in our place because He was made sin for us. Through His death upon the cross, we were made "alive in Him." Our very life is possible only through His death. Through His death, He conquered sin, Satan, Hell, and the Grave. He became weak, so we can be strong. He became sin so we can be righteous.

He became sick, so we can be healthy. He freed us from all the curses of spiritual death.

We became one with Him as He became one with us. If you would like to know my Master, study God's word, and pray in the spirit, constantly. He tells us, "If you draw near to me, I will draw near to you." Psalm 73:28(K J V), "But as for me, it is good for me to draw near to God; I have made the Lord God my refuge and placed my trust in Him that I may tell of all Your works." If you want to know the Master and His love, always remember He wants to know you just as much, even more. Just reach out to Him. Just whisper the name of Jesus, Amen! Romans 8:38-39 "For I am convinced [and continue to be convinced—beyond any doubt] that neither death, nor life, nor angels, nor principalities, nor things present and threatening, nor things to come, nor powers, 39 nor height, nor depth, nor any other created thing, will be able to separate us from the [unlimited] love of God, which is in Christ Jesus our Lord."

They say to know someone is to walk a mile in their shoes or in this case, sandals. To know our Master is to be the hands and feet of Jesus in this world. As I have said so many times, there is nothing you can do to make God love you anymore, and there's nothing you can do to make Him love you any less. Remember, He knew us before we were formed in our mother's womb. (Psalm 139:15) You are so very precious in His sight. Look what the Word has to say about each and every one of us in, Ephesians 2:10 "For we are his workmanship, created in Christ Jesus unto good works, which God hath before ordained that we should walk in them." Amen!

My prayer for each and every one of us is that we can say, yes, I know the Master and He knows me. If you don't know my Jesus, I would be happy to introduce Him to you. Amen!

November 4/2016
Rev Bruce Pero

CHAPTER 25
The Lamb of God

The parable of the King's son's Marriage Feast: Matthew 22:1-10 Jesus spoke to them again in parables, saying: 2 "The kingdom of heaven is like a king who prepared a wedding banquet for his son. 3 He sent his servants to those who had been invited to the banquet to tell them to come, but they refused to come. (We in today's world can look at this as though someone has preached the word of God to a congregation in a church and invited the people after the sermon to make their lives right with the Lord, by receiving their salvation but they refused it and walked away from God.) 4 "Then he sent some more servants (isn't this like our Heavenly Father to not give up on us) and said, 'Tell those who have been invited that I have prepared my dinner: My oxen and fattened cattle have been butchered, and everything is ready. Come to the wedding banquet.' (In this God is pleading with us to come). 5 "But they paid no attention and went off—one to his field, another to his business. 6 The rest seized his servants, mistreated them, and killed them." (This is also exactly what happened to the children of Israel when God continually invited them to join Him as His chosen people, the apple of God's eye. But they rejected Him as their messiah and went so far as to have Jesus crucified on the cross, totally rejecting Him to this very day. 7 The king was enraged. He sent his army and destroyed those murderers and burned their city. 8 "Then he said to his servants, 'The wedding banquet is ready, but those I invited did not deserve to come. 9 So go to the street corners and invite to the banquet anyone you find.'

(This can be looked at in this parable as when the Jews rejected Jesus, so He invited the gentiles to make the Jews jealous, to draw them back to serve and accept Jesus as their Messiah.

10 "So the servants went out into the streets and gathered all the people they could find, the bad as well as the good, and the wedding hall was filled with guests." Also in this parable, I believe Jesus was referring to the marriage supper of the Lamb, in that God has prepared a mighty banquet. Then He sent out His servants all the disciples, apostles, preachers, evangelists, and teachers to invite the guests to come. First the Jews, and when they had refused, He sent the invitation out this time to the gentiles, being you and me. I believe that will be one of the most glorious days where His word says that "every knee shall bend and every head shall bow." Then we march into the marriage supper of the Lamb where the church is arrayed in her most beautiful white linens and fine silks to meet the King of Kings and the Lord of Lords face to face; I look forward to that day more and more as life goes on. AMEN.

Let us turn in our Bibles to Revelation 19:7-9 Let us be glad and rejoice and give honor to Him: for the marriage of the

Lamb is come and his wife hath made herself ready. (Being the church) 8 Fine linen, bright and clean was given her to wear." (Fine linen stands for the righteous acts of God's holy people.) 9 Then the angel said to me, "Write this: Blessed are those who are invited to the wedding supper of the Lamb!" And he added, "These are the true words of God." Matthew 22:11-14 "But when the king came in to see the guests, he noticed a man there who was not wearing wedding clothes. 12 He asked, 'How did you get in here without wedding clothes, friend?' The man was speechless.13 "Then the king told the attendants, 'Tie him hand and foot, and throw him outside, into the darkness, where there will be weeping and gnashing of teeth.'

14 "For many are invited, but few are chosen." Over the years people have tried to lead us to believe that there are many ways to get into Heaven. I believe that when Jesus questioned the man who came to the wedding not prepared he was rejected. Remember, Jesus is teaching with a parable referring to the Wedding Supper of the Lamb. In verse 14 when it says many are invited, means many people are invited to Heaven for the Wedding Supper of the Lamb by the Holy Spirit. Because these people have not truly prepared their hearts for heaven,(the marriage super or union with Jesus, they will not be chosen to enter Heaven.) In other words, if we try to get into Heaven any other way than what the word tells us, we are not going to make it.

In John 14:6 the word Jesus saith unto him, (referring to Thomas) "I am the way, the truth, and the life: no man cometh unto the Father, but by me." In summing this up, God has through His Holy Spirit invited each one of us and so many other people to accept the invitation to the Marriage Supper of the Lamb and our heavenly reward and home with Him. But for whatever reasons people have turned Him down and will not change their lives. You see, in these days, people have everything they need. They do not have to rely on the favor of God to put food on the table, clothes on their backs, a roof over their heads, and a new car in the driveway.

The only time people call out to God is when their world comes crashing down around them. They lose their jobs, they lose their homes, they get a bad report from the doctor, then they come crying to our Heavenly Father for His help. If they would live their lives with Christ in them every day, a lot of their problems would not happen. AMEN. This brings us to the part where few are chosen because if we refuse to receive Christ's invitation into our lives then we cannot be chosen to be a part of His Heavenly Kingdom, to live out eternity with Him. AMEN. But remember there is nothing you can do to make your Heavenly Father love you any less, and there is nothing we can do to make Him love us anymore.

When you hear that call or feel that nudge of the Holy Spirit on your life, do not hesitate to answer the call. Throw your hands in the air and say, "Yes Lord, yes Lord, here I am what can I do for you?" Jesus loves us so much He is always waiting with His hand reaching out for us. If we will meet Him halfway, He will do the rest.

AMEN.

Bruce Pero
February 15, 2013

CHAPTER 26
Overcoming the Weakness of Fear of Sickness

October 1ST. 2008 While sitting in Tim Horton's with a friend I had a stroke behind my left eye. Some would ask what does that entail? Well, it means that the main blood vessel supplying blood to my eye burst. The doctor's report was that if I had been sitting in the hospital, they could not have fixed it. Thus I lost most of the vision in my eye. But you know I test it every day to see if it's healed and I believe one day it will be healed, either here or in Heaven. Amen!! Then on December 1ST. 2008 I was diagnosed with throat cancer. I thought, Lord if you are trying to get my attention you have my undivided attention. I know that is not how God works, but you know when this happened it took away many things in my life that were very meaningless, trivial, and were of no use to me in my walk with the Lord.

It caused me to step back and re-evaluate my life and my walk with Him. You have heard me say, I would not have wanted to miss this time, not because of the pain and suffering I went through, but for the experience and the intimacy that I was allowed to have with my Heavenly Father, and I still experience that same intimacy today. He wants the same for everyone if we will just allow it to happen and be open to it. But for whatever reason, we pull away, or get so wrapped up in the things around us, that we don't take the time to heed His word that tells us to, "Be still and know that I am God."

We need to stop and listen for that still small voice for direction in our lives; you know we can talk to Him just like we talk to our earthly fathers. We may not always like or understand the answers we get but He will speak to us through a direct answer or through His word.

2 Corinthians 12:8-10 "For this thing I besought the Lord thrice, that it might depart from me. 9 And He said unto me, my grace is sufficient for thee: for my strength is made perfect in weakness. Most gladly therefore will I rather glory in my infirmities, that the power of Christ may rest upon me." 10 Therefore I take pleasure in infirmities, in reproaches, in necessities, in persecutions, in distresses for Christ's sake: for when I am weak, then I am strong."

Weakness and self-confidence.

From the time I was very young, I could not get up in front of people to speak or share anything. But in August 2008, my brother and I started a Bible study and prayer meeting in Kingston, Ontario. It went well because my brother did all the talking. Then it came time for him to return to Korea, so he asked me to take over the meetings. I said," sure." Then I thought, what have I just committed to. Now I will have to do the talking.

But I had made a commitment to the Lord that if He opened the doors for me to minister, I would go through them, believing He would be with me. So, I went to the next meeting by myself and when I started to speak the Holy Spirit took over, I have never had a problem speaking to this day.

Mark 10:27 "Jesus looks at them and said, with man this is impossible, but with God; all things are possible."

2 Corinthians 9:8 "And God can make all Grace abound to you, so that in all things, at all times, having all that you need, you will abound in every good work." (One of the most profound words we need to remember is that God's Grace and Mercies are renewed each day. Jesus said in, 2 Timothy 1;7"For God did not give us a spirit of timidity or cowardice or fear, but [He has given us a spirit] of power and of love and of sound judgment and personal discipline [abilities that result in a calm, well-balanced mind and self-control]."

Hebrews 13:5"Let your conversation be without covetousness; and be content with such things as ye have: for he hath said, I will never leave thee, nor forsake thee."

You see, in our lives, we are going to have trials and tribulations; we are going to lose our loved ones, we are going to lose our best friend but just remember what God's word says in these last two scriptures.

"He did not give us a spirit of fear and He will never leave us or forsake us." At the time of our trials and tribulation, God is just a breath away. I know because I lived through these hard times like many of my friends and acquaintances.

As difficult as it may seem, trust me, the God I know has always been there in my darkest times. Blessings!

Revised in 01/22/22
Rev Bruce Pero

CHAPTER 27
Abandoned But Not Forsaken

It is hard to imagine seeing a little five-year-old man standing with his nose pressed against the glass watching dad leaving the driveway. Then you hear him ask, "Why is daddy leaving, doesn't he want to live here anymore, doesn't he love us anymore?" So many times, these little ones ask these questions with no one to answer them, because the grownups are so wrapped up in their own hurts, they don't see the hurts of the little ones.

Matthew 18:6 "But whoever causes one of these little ones who believe in Me to stumble and sin [by leading him away from My teaching], it would be better for him to have a heavy millstone [as large as one turned by a donkey] hung around his neck and to be drowned in the depth of the sea."

So, what do you mean by stumbling? Well I'm glad you asked. When we think of only our problems, and the situations we are going through, not realizing those little people God has blessed us with are going to suffer just as much and maybe more. We try to cope with divorce, separation, and deaths in the family; those little ones have to deal with the same situations as we do at the same time. Sometimes the side- effects for them can last a lifetime, also quite often can destroy their life.

People quite often forget that these little ones are a gift from God and should be taken care of as such. Grownups get so wrapped up in their personal cares and lives that the children take second place if they find any place in their parent's hearts at all. Young couples, when they decide to get married need to take some time and decide what role their children are going to play in their lives. Remembering, they are not just another fixture in the scheme of things, or another possession, another accomplishment.

I used to tell people that children to parents are like having puppy syndrome. What does that mean? People get puppies thinking they are so cute and cuddly until they grow up. Then they have to be fed, walked and trained, cleaned up after, and taken care of.

In the same context, our children when they are born are cute and cuddly. Then the time comes to raise them and teach them the things of life. In both cases, there comes responsibility. That's when, quite often, they are abandoned and forsaken to make their own way through life. I am sure Jesus would weep as He did in the Garden of Gethsemane to see this taking place.

Matthew 10:21 "Brother will betray brother to death, and the father his child; and children will rise up and rebel against their parents and cause them to be put to death." Matthew

15:26And He replied, "It is not good (appropriate, fair) to take the children's bread and throw it to the pet dogs."

From the beginning of time, our Heavenly Father has referred to you and me as His children. Even after all the sins that were committed by the people of the world, God's love for the people He created never failed.

Mark 10:14 But when Jesus saw this, He was indignant and He said to them, "Allow the children to come to Me; do not forbid them; for the kingdom of God belongs to such as these."

If we remember the story in the Bible where the little children were crowding Jesus, the disciples came and tried to shew the children away thinking they were disturbing Jesus. Jesus said, "Let them stay for this is what heaven is going to be like." We will all be His children never to be abandoned.

Let your character or moral disposition be free from love of money [including greed, avarice, lust, and craving for earthly possessions] and be satisfied with your present [circumstances and with what you have]; for He [God] Himself has said, "I will not in any way fail you nor give you up nor leave you without support.

[I will] not, [I will] not, [I will] not in any degree leave you helpless nor forsake nor let [you] down (relax My hold on you)!"

Hebrews 13:5

So, parents before we run off to the divorce court, and become separated from each other, think about the life you started out with, and how much in love you were. Then if you have children think of the effect it will leave on their lives. We sometimes can become so selfish that we only think about ourselves and what we are going through right now.

It's time we stopped letting small issues build up until they are totally out of control. I have always believed that communication in the marriage was the next item on our list right after Love.

Most marriages ended with promises for better or for worse. Then the minister ended everything with a prayer of blessing the couple and their marriage. The line for better or worse is a promise that we will never abandon or forsake each other. But too many times we do just that and run away, thinking that life has to be better somewhere else. We also abandon the blessing over our lives the minister prayed for us. So even though we abandoned each other and our children, God made a promise never to leave us or abandon us and He has kept that promise; He loves each and every one of us.

Jesus spoke His truth when He said, John 3:17 "For God did not send His Son into the world to judge (to reject, to condemn, to pass sentence on) the world, but that the world might find salvation and be made safe and sound in Him."

Shortly, I am expecting to attend a new wedding supper.

Its proper name is the Marriage Supper of the Lamb when we will be united with our Lord and Savior. That will be a happy day for all who know Jesus as their Lord and Savior. So, you see we abandon, Spouses, Children, Family, and Friends, but we are never abandoned or forsaken by Jesus because He loves us so much, He only wants the very best for all His children.

So, I ask you in closing before you make those difficult decisions in your life that will have a tremendous effect and outcome on you and others around you, take it to the Lord. He is a very good listener and believe it or not, He hears everything you say. He may not answer right away or give you the answer you expected but He will answer you. Perhaps it won't be the answer you were looking for, but it will only be for the best because He only gives His children what is good.

If you are feeling abandoned or forsaken why not ask Jesus to come to be your Lord and Savior. Give Him control of your life. You have tried everything else. He won't let you down. Amen!!!

May 7/2022
Rev Bruce Pero

CHAPTER 28
The Holy Spirit is in You

Many times, when we gather in our church services, we read a few verses in God's word. Then we tend to show how it applies to our everyday lives, which is good because God wants us to learn His word and how we can apply it. But there is so much more God wants from us. He wants us to walk in the Spirit.

John 4:23 "But a time is coming and is already here when the true worshipers will worship the Father in spirit [from the heart, the inner self] and in truth; for the Father seeks such people to be His worshipers." Jesus said, "I only do what the Father tells me."

John 5:19 So Jesus answered them by saying, "I assure you and most solemnly say to you, the Son can do nothing of Himself [of His own accord], unless it is something He sees the Father doing; for whatever things the Father does, the Son [in His turn] also does in the same way."

John 6:63 "It is the Spirit that quickened; the flesh profits nothing: the words that I speak unto you, they are spirit, and they are life."

The words we speak through, or from the Holy Spirit are the very heartbeat of God. Matthew 10:7 And as ye go, preach, saying, "The kingdom of heaven is at hand." This is to say that we have the Father, Son, and Holy Spirit in us as we carry the very presence of Heaven by being the doorway to Heaven. The purpose of life is to bring Heaven and earth together. When you speak, words become Spirit.

John 6:26-27 Jesus answered, "I assure you and most solemnly say to you, you have been searching for Me, not because you saw the signs (attesting miracles), but because you ate the loaves and were filled."

27 "Do not work for food that perishes, but for food that endures [and leads] to eternal life, which the Son of Man will give you; for God the Father has authorized Him and put His seal on Him." (Remember what the Father spoke over Jesus when Jesus was baptized by John the Baptist. Matthew 3:16-17 "After Jesus was baptized, He came up immediately out of the water; and behold, the heavens were opened, and he (John) saw the Spirit of God descending as a dove and lighting on Him (Jesus), 17 Behold, a voice from heaven said, "This is My beloved Son, in whom I am well-pleased and delighted!"

A prayer we should pray often is, to open the Heaven over our cities and allow the Holy Spirit to take control and move in our lives. Prayer for Mercy and Help Isaiah 64:1-4 "Oh, that You would tear open the heavens (rend the Heavens) and come down.

That the mountains might quake at Your presence—

2 As [sure as] fire kindles the brushwood, as fire causes water to boil

to make Your name known to Your adversaries, That the nations may tremble at Your presence!

3 When You did awesome and amazing things which we did not expect, you came down [at Sinai]; the mountains quaked at Your presence.

4 For from days of old no one has heard, nor has ear perceived,

nor has the eye seen a God besides You, who works and acts on behalf of the one who [gladly] waits for Him."

Don't grieve the Holy Spirit, by not allowing Him to move and operate in our daily lives. Also do not quench the Holy Spirit, when the Holy Spirit is moving. Do not stop the moving of the Holy Spirit.

Jesus is looking for a generation to display purity and holiness. The Holy Spirit is burning in us wanting to get out to manifest the glory of Jesus as our Lord and Savior, to win lost souls to Him.

Churches today gather around the scriptures. Israel gathered around the Holy Spirit. It is all well and good to study the scriptures; but people need to function at a higher level and operate through the Holy Spirit, living their lives as Jesus did.

John 4:23 "But a time is coming and is already here when the true worshipers will worship the Father in spirit [from the heart, the inner self] and in truth; for the Father seeks such people to be His worshipers."

When you walk daily in the Spirit you will find out that every believer has an open Heaven over them. You have the authority and power to call down the Holy Spirit upon your cities, communities, families, and friends, to operate in the way God intended for our lives to be. When you walk filled with the presence of the Holy Spirit you will operate as Jesus did. When Jesus was walking through the crowded streets there was a woman with the issue of blood that pressed through the crowd. She reached out and touched the hem of His garment because she had faith that if she could touch Him, she would be healed. Jesus said, "Who touched me?" because He felt the power leave His body. His disciples said, "Master there are so many people pressing in, how would we know who touched you?" Jesus replied, "I felt the virtue or power leave me." Matthew 9:20-22 "Then a woman who had suffered from a hemorrhage for twelve years came up behind Him and touched the [tassel] fringe of His outer robe; 21 for she had been saying to herself, "If I only touch His outer robe, I will be healed."

22 But Jesus turning and seeing her said, "Take courage, daughter; your [personal trust and confident] faith [in Me] has made you well." And at once the woman was [completely] healed.

In closing, you too can walk with that same Holy Spirit anointing if you only press into His Presence, the same power that flowed through Jesus is available for you and me. It is called walking daily in the Spirit.

When you pray for anyone, you too can sense the power or spiritual virtue that leaves you as Jesus did. To walk in this presence of anointing is a gift from our Heavenly Father.

Remember to get to this point we are all called to praise and worship our Lord in spirit and in truth. Psalm 150 "Praise ye the Lord. Praise God in his sanctuary: praise him in the firmament of his power. 2 Praise him for his mighty acts: praise him according to his excellent greatness.   3 Praise him with the sound of the trumpet: praise him with the psaltery and harp. 4 Praise him with the timbrel and dance: praise him with stringed instruments and organs. 5 Praise him upon the loud cymbals: praise him upon the high-sounding cymbals. 6 Let everything that hath breath praise the Lord. Praise ye the Lord."

He inhabits the praise of His people that is why praise is our assignment on earth. God doesn't care how it sounds to make a joyful noise unto the Lord. Remember God inhabits our praises. Amen!

November 30,2022
Rev Bruce Pero